BEFORE THE BOOM

*Latin American Revolutionary Novels
of the 1920s*

Elizabeth Coonrod Martínez

University Press of America,® Inc.
Lanham · New York · Oxford

Copyright © 2001 by
University Press of America,® Inc.
4720 Boston Way
Lanham, Maryland 20706

12 Hid's Copse Rd.
Cumnor Hill, Oxford OX2 9JJ

Library of Congress Cataloging-in-Publication Data

Martínez, Elizabeth Coonrod.
Before the Boom : Latin American revolutionary novels of the
1920s / Elizabeth Coonrod Martínez.
p.   cm
Includes bibliographical references and index.
1. Spanish American fiction—20th century—History and criticism.
2. Experimental fiction, Spanish American—History and criticism.
3. Vela, Arqueles, 1899- Café de nadie. 4. Arlt, Roberto, 1900-1942.
Siete locos. 5. Palacio, Pablo. Dâbora. 6. Adân, Martân, 1908- Casa de
cartân. I. Title.
PQ7082.N7 M347   2001   863'.640998—dc21   00-068317 CIP

ISBN 0-7618-1948-7 (pbk. : alk. paper)

⊖™ The paper used in this publication meets the minimum
requirements of American National Standard for Information
Sciences—Permanence of Paper for Printed Library Materials,
ANSI Z39.48—1984

I have been blessed with two beautiful, wonderful sisters,
to whom this book is dedicated:

To the memory of Letitia Sue (1942-2000)
and for
Elena Isabel

CONTENTS

Preface

This book is designed to introduce English readers to the period of radical innovation in Latin American narrative fiction which occurred shortly after the turn of the twentieth century, known in Spanish as *Vanguardia*. Little has been published on the literature of this period in English-language texts, and yet it is an important moment for Latin American literature, just as it was for English-language and European literature (in English, and also in Brazil, this literary period is called Modernism). Latin American revolutionary novels produced early in the twentieth century, and in opposition to Realism and Romanticism, have been for the most part forgotten and overshadowed by the later, world-famous "Boom" generation of the 1960s. Although not clearly identified as a literary generation, the Latin American Vanguardia was rich in innovation and technique. This period's theater and poetry have received more critical attention and interest. Vanguardia prose fiction, however, responded to a universal call for not only social and political but also artistic rebellion against a norm that was changing with each new scientific, technological and philosophical discovery. It is an exciting period in fiction.

The Vanguardia novel has been neglected by critics and classrooms of the late twentieth century, and only recently has been considered for its impact on the later novel. Members of the Latin American Boom considered *themselves* the innovators, declaring they had no "father" of influence. Recently, critics have given some credit for influence on Boom novelists to writers of the late 1930s and 1940s rather than the earlier Vanguardia groups. Now, postmodern theory provides an excellent opportunity for a re-reading of these early, innovative artists. The questioning of master narratives, and a view from outside the center, help to see the reasons behind the radical form and revolutionary style of such early, innovative Latin American narrative.

In this study of four novels of the 1920s, Arqueles Vela's *El café de nadie* (Mexico), Roberto Arlt's *Los siete locos* (Argentina), Pablo Palacio's *Débora* (Ecuador), and Martín Adán's *La casa de cartón* (Peru), I attempt to demonstrate some forerunners of Boom fiction and the contemporary Latin American novel. There is a story behind the creation of each novel—a socio-political, historical setting—that is important to artistic production in the Vanguardia. From this groundwork, readers can embark on further study of pre-Boom Latin American narrative fiction. Only in recent years have specific critical studies been published on the Latin American Vanguardia, and mostly in Spanish. My hope is that this text will make English-language readers curious and interested in Latin American writers of the early twentieth century, and their place as innovators of modern fiction—the true rebels in search of a new art and a new novel.

Vela, Arlt, Palacio, and Adán's novels do what Boom novelists would later receive credit for: begin the distortion in structure and content of a novel; express an idea rather than a story; and use examples and images rather than characters. These early novels have been overshadowed and ignored due to assessments that they were non-novels, not well-written or well-constructed. Now they can be re-examined, and enjoyed, for what they accomplished.

Vanguardia narrative distorted, parodied and challenged, the universal and the Latin American novel to open new discourse and new narrative form. Later generations of Latin American writers owe a debt to these writers of revolutionary creativity.

Acknowledgments

Since no work is possible without the support and influence of the community and people around you, I am immensely grateful to all who have inspired and helped make possible the publication of this book.

A principal mentor in the creation of this project is Dick Gerdes. His solid guidance and encouragement helped keep the manuscript within a reasonable size and scope, and I am grateful for his patient reading and comments. I am grateful for Tey Diana Rebolledo's insight, and patient reading on my manuscript, and the inspiration that she provided early on when she required her graduate students to *perform* their understanding of the avant-garde movements. I would like to thank Ruth Salvaggio for introducing me to such theorists as Trinh Minh-ha, Patricia J. Williams, and Donna Haraway. Several people were excellent listeners and readers in the final stages of this manuscript, to whom I am especially appreciative, my sister Elena, Fern and Arturo Ramírez, and Francisco Vázquez.

It is from my students that I draw much of my enthusiasm for commentary on Latin American literature, and I am thankful to the many wonderful students in my classes at Sonoma State University, who have inspired me with their own enthusiasm and who allow me to share my love of literature and Latin American culture in their lives.

I appreciate the support of Robert West at UPA, for his belief in my ideas and his continued encouragement toward the publication of this book.

The research for this project was supported in part by two fellowships from Sonoma State University, which I acknowledge with gratitude: The Research, Scholarship and Creative Activity Projects (RSCAP) awards for the summers of 1997 and 1998, afforded me the opportunity to dedicate those summers to completion of research and some of the writing of this book.

A portion of Chapter 5, titled, "Back to the Future in Vanguardia Narrative: Martín Adán's Vision and Revisioning of the New Era," appeared in the first issue of *Corner* (Fall 1998), an electronic, online journal dedicated to the avant-garde. My original ideas for Chapter 2 appeared in a short essay titled, "Mexico's First Rebellious Novel: Futurism and Arqueles Vela's *El café de nadie*," in *The Image of Technology in Literature, the Media, and Society* (1994).

A good faith effort was made to reach publishers of Pablo Palacio's and Martín Adán's novels, to no avail.

The following have generously given permission to use extended quotations from their copyrighted works: Publisher Editorial Losada, S.A., in Buenos Aires, for quotations from *Los siete locos*, by Roberto Arlt (6th ed., 1985), and translator Katherine Silver, for use of quotations from her English translation of Martín Adán's novel, *The Cardboard House*, published by Graywolf Press.

The *great* war, which was to have made
the world safe for democracy, succeeded
far better in making the world safe for
the artistic avant-garde... World War I
indirectly advanced the cause of
modernism in the promise that a new
order was at hand.

-Roger Shattuck[1]

INTRODUCTION:
AN EXCITING AND TUMULTUOUS ERA

In the beginning of this century, Latin America gave birth to a rich
profusion of innovative narrative fiction in an era equally rich in
technological and scientific innovation. But while the new novel of the
1920s replaced Romantic and Realist forms, its achievement has for the
most part been forgotten and overshadowed by the more-celebrated
novel of the Latin American "Boom"—so-called by critics who decided
that Latin American narrative *exploded* into existence in the 1960s and
early 1970s, to the acclaim of international readers. The inception of a
new style of writing, and much of the preparation of innovative
narrative form, actually occurred in a previous generation, *before* the
Boom. The Latin American *Vanguardia* extended from as early as the
second decade of the twentieth century to as late as the 1940s, with
principal works dating from 1922 to 1930. Vanguardia artists were
actively involved in their societies, and responded to a call for universal
social and political change; prose writers reinvented the novel to keep
up with new developments in science, philosophy, and politics that
marked the new century. However, fiction of this period is
remembered mainly for its Realism focused on specific regions:
Ricardo Guiraldes' *Don Segundo Sombra* (1926), Rómulo Gallegos'
Doña Bárbara (1929), and the novels of the Mexican Revolution such
as Martín Luis Guzmán's *El águila y la serpiente* (1928). The few
Vanguardia studies have tended to focus on poetry, and innovative
Vanguardia poets such as Vicente Huidobro, César Vallejo, José

Gorostiza or Delmira Agustini are noted for their experimental language, while the Vanguardia novelists—who reinvented the novel—have been mostly forgotten.

Recent turns in postmodern literary theory offer a unique opportunity to re-evaluate narrative fiction in the third decade of the twentieth century for its influence on the evolution of the Latin American novel. This study proposes to discuss four revolutionary Latin American novels from Mexico, Argentina, Ecuador, and Peru which forever altered and renovated narrative form, and achieved a discourse little understood in their era. The 1960s "Boom" is considered the Latin American golden era for narrative fiction, but some of its traits can be found in the 1920s Vanguardia novels. They are precursors to the Boom literature, and to the so-called postmodern novel of the late 1970s and 1980s. The following chapters include a thorough analysis of Arqueles Vela's *El café de nadie* (Mexico, 1926); Roberto Arlt's *Los siete locos* (Argentina, 1929); Pablo Palacio's *Débora* (Ecuador, 1927); and Martín Adán's *La casa de cartón* (Peru, 1928). Each of these four novels breaks with traditional literature content and structure when many other novelists were writing within the realist/naturalist tradition, popular in Latin America following its earlier surge in Europe. Because of the public's preference for mainstream writing, Vanguardia narrative was overlooked (and these novels remained out-of-print) until recent reviews of the period. Until recently, poets were considered the major innovators before the Boom period.

Argentinian Jorge Luis Borges (1889-1986) has long been cited as a precursor to Latin American Boom fiction, and more recently Chilean María Luisa Bombal (1910-1980) has been hailed as another significant influence (Agosín 28). This study attempts to show that the creative work of Vanguardia novelists, in their specific socio-historic situations, laid the groundwork—before Borges and others—for the narrative production that followed. It also demonstrates that Latin American writers of this era were as revolutionary in their ideas as European writers of the same era, while also seeking to express their *American* experience.

This is not to state that these novels are the only innovators or precursors to the Boom. However, they can provide a foundation for rereading other novels of the period, often called only *fragments* or experiments by critics. There is a need to examine why critics and novelists cite Boom fiction (with an occasional precursor) as the *first flowering* of the new Latin American novel of the twentieth century.

The principal Boom novelists declared themselves an "orphan" generation, with no universal Latin American "father" of influence

(Donoso 20), which supposedly emerged as the first generation of real Latin American novelists. Doris Sommer pinpoints the fallacy of this idea, showing that while Mario Vargas Llosa (1936-) says he sought to be "modern" and "different," he acknowledged that this desire fed from an existing tradition of experimentation (Sommer 3-4). Indeed, revolutionary style, and modernity are the obvious traits of the Vanguardia novels, and were part of a tradition begun long before the Boom's inception.

The Latin American Vanguardia corresponds to Modernism in the United States and Europe. The Modernists were innovative poets and writers such as Ezra Pound, James Joyce, and T.S. Eliot, who gained their fame in the 1920s. The production of these artistic revolutionary writers was more astringent and uncompromising in the second decade of the twentieth century (Bradbury 158), and then exploded in the 1920s. In London, revolutionary writers gained their fame in the 1920s and 1930s. European avant-garde poets launched their rebellion during the First World War (1914-18); their manifestos attracted prose writers by the early 1920s who explored new forms of narrative throughout the decade. In Latin America, poets explored innovative form and language as early as 1916, and first published their new style in the 1920s. César Vallejo's *Trilce* (1922), for example, could have influenced Vanguardia novelists; but other Latin American poets achieved significant creations *after* the breakthroughs of narrative fiction, namely Vicente Huidobro's *Altazor* (1931). Obviously, novelists and poets were creating simultaneously in the Vanguardia era.

The last two decades of the nineteenth century saw an incredible move from rural to urban life in many countries, leading to new jobs and better access to literary culture. The half-century before World War I was the most remarkable period of economic growth in history, not excluding the latter part of the twentieth century (Bullock 59). During this period, European capitals—Paris, London, Berlin—were the centers of huge networks of industry, commerce, and finance. The rise of an international economy was a direct result of both great industrial expansion in the 1890s and a technological revolution at the turn of the century, which led to key developments: the internal combustion engine, the diesel engine, and the steam turbine; electricity, oil, and petroleum as new sources of power; the automobile, the tractor, the motor bus, and the aeroplane; the telephone, the typewriter, and the tape machine (the foundation of modern office organization); and the production of synthetic materials.

By 1900, eleven metropolises in the world boasted populations of more than a million (by 1910, London, New York, and Mexico City had populations of more than five million). Availability of reading materials and an enormous increase in literacy provided an avenue for a revolution in language by the second decade of this century. Positivism and Rationalism would be replaced by radical new ways of thought which also influenced writers. Compared to the long realm of Realism or Romanticism in the previous century, Europe's revolutionary artistic movements—Cubism (1907), Futurism (1909), Stravinsky's atonal music (1909), Dadaism (1916), Apollinaire's literary cubism (1914), German expressionism (1911), Pound's imaginism (1912), and Surrealism (1924)—quickly influenced and affected writers throughout the literary world. The impetus for artistic revolution arose mostly out of rapidly advancing scientific thought (primarily the Theory of Relativity), the new study of psychoanalysis, and an artistic desire to move away from the French Decadents' concern with vice and unnaturalness at the close of the nineteenth century (Shattuck 344). Writers were also influenced by new ideologies, such as Fascism and Marxism, which gained interest in Latin American countries after the Russian Revolution of 1917 and World War I.

Avant-garde artists were influenced by a quickly changing technological society, which made people more aware of and dependent on each other. In 1903, Orville Wright's debut in the air led to the manufacture of numerous types of war planes during World War I. In 1904, modern business tactics were born in Max Weber's essay, *The Protestant Ethic and the Spirit of Capitalism*. The first music was transmitted by radio in Austria, and work began on the Panama Canal in 1904. Neon lights arrived in 1905 along with Albert Einstein's first Theories on Relativity (he published his general theories on relativity in 1915), and the first bus system appeared on London streets (taxis appeared in London in 1903).In 1906 the first color movie and the first modern battleship made their debuts. Scientists discovered tissue culture, chemistry of proteins, and commercial plastic. The fountain pen was invented in 1908, altering the process of writing, and permanent waves were first given in 1909, thus changing hair styling. Technology affected music and painting, while the world was growing smaller and more accessible with faster methods of transportation and communication.

Life was also speeding up. In 1910 Barney Oldfield set an automobile speed record of 133 miles per hour. People regularly crossed the Atlantic Ocean in large dirigibles. The world was becoming a strange place, with worldwide communication not only affecting how life was lived but also artistic production.

So how did narrative fiction respond to life in this era? Thought and artistic expression had evolved in the late nineteenth century under Sigmund Freud's influence. His *Interpretation of Dreams* (1900) led artists to automatic writing, a subconscious reaction that was explained as more real than tangible reality. In art, Pablo Picasso's painting *Les Demoiselles d'Avignon* (1907) radically broke with tradition in its representation of the human form, and the master of new theater, Bertolt Brecht, wanted the audience to think rather than identify; he said visual reality was not necessarily the Truth. Realism—the advocacy of verisimilitude in mid-nineteenth century France which flourished in the revolutionary scientific confidence of that era—no longer fit with a new reality. Avant-garde artists found themselves in a world of chaos and sought to reconcile fantasy and logic, and to find ways to explain a truer reality of the moment. Their style would be as chaotic as the unstable human situation in which they found themselves.

In Latin America, the first two decades of the century were equally a period of turmoil and again rapid technological and political change. After a century of independence from Spain, Latin Americans were beginning to become more aware of each other and of the rapidly changing world at large. Then the 1920s surged dramatically toward economic collapse by 1929. Artists sought various ways to describe the economic and social turmoil of their era. In Mexico, the *indigenista* and the political/documentary novels of the 1910 Revolution reached their height in this period, but were based on conventional structures. Latin American *Modernismo* (1880-1910; closely related to European Parnassian and Decadent movements [*l'art pour l'art*]) had essentially won the esthetic battle in its revolution, and there was no reason for the artist of the 1920s to repeat it (Anderson Imbert 11). Still, some artists attempted new esthetic approaches using a more universal language than the self-involved *Modernistas*. Chile's Vicente Huidobro (1893-1948) led the *Creacionismo* movement in Spain in 1918, and believed the artist was none other than a god in his creative power (an idea somewhat similar to that of Russian Modernists, who viewed art as a creative force destined to create not artistic texts, but life itself). By 1920, Argentina's Jorge Luis Borges (who had been in Spain) would take his literary movement, *Ultraísmo*, to Latin America. The Ultraists incorporated current European artistic trends and sought to sensationalize the metaphor, or push it to its limit. Artists especially wanted to diverge from the Latin American Modernistas, whose introverted search for supreme beauty had fallen on deaf ears. At this time, two principal literary currents predominated in Spanish America: one with a politically committed, or nationalistic content, and the other purely esthetic. Neither produced novels that attracted worldwide attention or revolutionized Latin American narrative.

Operating alone in Latin America, the Vanguardia novelists broke new terrain by undoing traditional narrative structure, showing the process of artistic creation, and emphasizing the need for a new novel. While they received some critical attention, they were mainly considered strange. However, they are the true predecessors of the modern novel—including the Boom novel—a fact that is only recently beginning to be recognized in critical texts.

Contemporary critical theory allows for re-readings of earlier narrative texts, including the hindsight not afforded the artists' contemporaries, and seeks to establish the importance of a genre and a specific historical period (Pérez Firmat 10). Little work has been done on Latin American avant-garde fiction, especially in English, but recently critics have begun to study its impact. The following are excellent sources in English.

An authoritative bibliography, *Vanguardism in Latin American Literature* (1990), was compiled by Merlin H. Forster with an eye to changing the impression that the Vanguardia movement consisted of "derivative experimentation that had little impact on subsequent developments" (7). In fact, Forster believes that the Vanguardia narrative production contributed directly to present-day, post-Boom or postmodern Latin American literature due to its similarity in a key concept that he calls a severance of "the accepted link between observable reality and artistic creation" (9).

Although published nearly two decades ago, Gustavo Pérez Firmat's book *Idle Fictions: The Hispanic Vanguard Novel, 1926-1934* (1982), is remarkably unique in that it examines only narrative works of the avant-garde in Spanish; however, he concentrates more heavily on Spain's rather than Latin America's contribution. The few Spanish-American writers he highlights, Jaime Torres Bodet (1902-1974) and Eduardo Mallea (1903-1982), are less radical than the novelists in this study. Pérez Firmat is also more interested in documenting the existence of a Vanguardia in Spanish language than the contributions of specific writers to the novel genre. He states that the debate surrounding Vanguardia fiction began in 1926 with a series of novels published by *Revista de Occidente* (8). The debate (to be discussed more fully in Chapter Two) was a direct result of Mexican poet Torres Bodet's rebuttal to José Ortega y Gasset's argument that the novel had entered into a period of crisis (5). Ortega y Gasset's *La deshumanización del arte e ideas sobre la novela* (1925) initiated an intellectual analysis in Spain decrying the "modern" novel (17).

While Pérez Firmat sees an argument between fossilized structures and an unrealized contemporary novel (4), he does not discuss the earliest stages of Vanguardia fiction in Latin America. Neither does he mention the Mexican *Estridentista* movement, which first issued a Vanguardia manifesto in 1921. The Estridentistas (principally Manuel Maples Arce, Germán List Arzubide, Salvador Gallardo, Luis Quintanilla, and Arqueles Vela) issued their second manifesto on January 1, 1923. They called for a production not "contaminated by a lethargic reactionism," but a young and enthusiastic art, structured differently, and exalting a modern thematics of machines and laborious explosions (Verani 94).

Instead, Pérez Firmat examines what could be called the second wave of Vanguardia, 1926 to 1934, which included critical reaction to incipient revolutionary fiction, such as Arqueles Vela's *El café de nadie*, published serially in 1922, 1924, and 1926 (see Chapter Two). Essays on the impact of new fiction began several years after this artistic break with traditional structure. The first wave occurred simultaneously in several cities. In Sao Paolo, Brazil, the avant-garde began in 1922 with the Semana de Arte Moderna. In London, innovative novels were published in 1922: Virginia Woolf's *Jacob's Room*, James Joyce's *Ulysses*, T.S. Eliot's *The Waste Land*, and Ezra Pound's *The Cantos*. Mexico's first avant-garde manifesto was read in 1921 in Mexico City, and the first part of Arqueles Vela's novel was published in 1922. The second Vanguardia wave consists of novels published in the second half of the 1920s. The final wave, according to some critics, occurred in the 1930s and 1940s, i.e., María Luisa Bombal's influential novels, *La última niebla* (1934) and *La amortajada* (1941), and Miguel Angel Asturias' early works.

A recent survey of contemporary Spanish American fiction by Naomi Lindstrom, *Twentieth Century Spanish American Fiction* (1994), includes a chapter on "avant-garde modes" (1920 to 1950), and notes the transition from the revolutionary Vanguardia to the magical realism of Miguel Angel Asturias (1899-1974) and Alejo Carpentier (1904-1980). Literature surveys prior to the 1990s have not included such a delineated category for Vanguardia. Lindstrom contends that the vanguardistas responded initially to the new technology by using abruptly shifting, telegraphic, helter-skelter images based on European avant-garde concepts but clearly set in urban Latin America (69). These concepts, in turn, influenced the Mexican *Contemporáneos* (who followed the Estridentistas) in the late 1920s and early 1930s. Theirs was an urban-based writing of emotional intensity and inventive qualities (72). The Contemporáneos valued personal expression, but they did not seek to radically alter narrative form like the Estridentistas did. In the early 1930s, Latin American writing turned to the "fantastic or expressionistic qualities" (79) of novelists whose youths (i.e., Ernesto Sábato) were marked by Surrealism (91). According to

Lindstrom, many characteristics of the Vanguardia movement became a part of the Latin American literary mainstream, through "the spread of avant-garde, fantastic or at least highly imaginative writing features into what would otherwise have been realistic writing" (108-109). In fact, she is one of the first critics to note a link between the early new novelists, such as Arqueles Vela, and later pre-Boom and Boom novelists, thus firmly establishing the impact of the Vanguardia: "The fiction of the boom represents, in a number of ways, the continuation of the avant-garde tendencies that arose in Spanish America in the 1920s" (142).

Before Ortega y Gassett and Torres Bodet debated the effectiveness of the new novel, writers in several Latin American countries were experimenting with form. They often began by reading a manifesto, generally published in a literary journal or newspaper (although in Brazil the call to arms was a weeklong event of manifestos and artistic exhibitions in 1922). In Argentina, Jorge Luis Borges published his first manifesto in 1920. The following year he launched the Ultraísmo movement, based on a term that Guillermo de Torre had coined in his book *Literaturas europeas de vanguardia* (1925). Torre's book is considered the first overview of new artistic trends in the Spanish-speaking countries (Anderson Imbert 15-16). Other Latin American writers were also declaring manifestos for a new art early in the 1920s. Therefore, while Ortega y Gassett decried the decadence of the novel, Latin American writers were already putting theory into practice; that is, beginning to use new, universal language, in poetry and narrative. While Borges searched for an exalted metaphor, others sought an explosion of impossible structures. Acclaimed *precursor* Borges and Contemporáneos writer Torres Bodet went on to produce poetic prose, but with traditional structures, while other artists defied traditional form, thus stimulating the birth of a new novel (as Mikhail Bakhtin correctly foresaw in his early theories).

Latin America's socio-economic situation in the 1920s was different from Europe. It was tired from revolution (i.e., Mexico), it had to deal with large migrations to the urban centers, and was teetering on the brink of economic collapse—facts never mentioned by Pérez Firmat in his study on the causes of Vanguardia. Some Latin American intellectuals traveled to Madrid and Paris where they studied new artistic trends, but they returned home to seek their own creative identities (much as Diego Rivera did with mural art in Mexico, after having lived 10 years in Paris). While European literary journals and manifestos provided direction, there was a "sharp awareness of being American, of ingesting and digesting European cultural values" (Forster 8) in order to create something expressly Latin American, in much the same manner as the Bloomsbury group in the Anglo-English tradition.

The language commonality in Spanish American and Spain Vanguardia narrative would seem to provide a logical grouping for a study; however, it is important to be aware of the differences between Spain and the Americas. Pérez Firmat does not address this in his study; his focus is principally on the existence of Spain's Vanguardia. The following is accomplished in his definitive study of Spanish-language avant-garde narrative: (1) he discusses less radical Latin American writers, such as Eduardo Mallea and Jaime Torres Bodet; (2) he centers his study on the Peninsular opinions on the esthetic rather than the discourse of Vanguardia fiction; and, finally, (3) his reading is not based on the realization of the modern novel, but on its exception from the mainstream. In fact, he concludes that "Vanguard fiction exists between parentheses" (139), and that its production was a "vacation," a playful period of literature (141). While this may or may not be true in Spain, in Latin America practicing parody was a revolutionary act. This artistic parody was interpreted as only playful art by some of the artists' peers, but others reacted in hostile fashion (as Pérez Firmat notes). Vanguardia novelists were misunderstood, but Postmodern perspectives help to discover their serious intentions.

While Pérez Firmat strives to measure reaction to an already developed avant-garde narrative by citing numerous newspaper reviews published in Spain, this study will attempt to reveal the Latin American perspective and concentrate on its initiators as well as the way Vanguardia discourse is achieved. Although Pérez Firmat affirms that the Vanguardia novel worked to occupy and recolonize conventional narrative terrain while taking power away from the old and the traditional (33), he does not discuss the real achievements of the Vanguardia novelists. According to Derridean theory everything is discourse, therefore this "play" with its seeming lack of structure and plot must have a serious intention. With the hindsight of postmodern times, it is easier to see that the Vanguardia artist was not committing anarchy so much as seeking a new vision, a personal poetics. The Vanguardia artist understood that nature/art could not be repeated or imitated any longer; now they had to find ways of creating literature as new and fast as technology.

It was a serious, rigorous endeavor. Vanguardia writers asked themselves difficult questions about the nature of art. They sought to make contact with readers and reveal an artistically defined self (Unruh 28-29). Many of the questions they raised continue to influence literary and theoretical discourse in present times, according to Vicky Unruh, whose book *Latin American Vanguards: The Art of Contentious*

Encounters (1994) is one of the most recent and thorough studies in English on this Latin American literary period. She examines the artists' interaction between art and experience, cites their contributions, and meticulously examines texts by many Vanguardia initiators, such as Roberto Arlt, Vicente Huidobro, Martín Adán and Brazilian Oswald de Andrade. She also cites Mexican novels by the Contemporáneos Jaime Torres Bodet and Xavier Villaurrutia. While Unruh's study is extremely helpful (like Pérez Firmat's a decade earlier) in identifying the forces that moved the Vanguardia artist to create, the study herein concentrates on the inception and a few forerunners of radical narrative: namely Arlt, Adán, Pablo Palacio and Arqueles Vela. The latter two novelists are not explored in Unruh's study, and she considers Arlt's earlier novel *El juguete rabioso*, 1927, rather than *Los siete locos*.

Another recent book that is helpful in providing a broad description of avant-garde activity in Latin America, although in Spanish, is Jorge Schwartz's *Las vanguardias latinoamericanas: Textos programáticos y críticos* (1991). His study provides a thorough history of activities during the first two to three decades of the twentieth century, examining artistic movements that impacted on literature, such as Futurism, Surrealism, and Expressionism. Mexican critic Octavio Paz (1914-) argues for the uniqueness of the twentieth-century Latin American Vanguardia in his book *Children of the Mire* (1974), but he sees connections with the previous century's Romanticism (102). Merlin Forster and Vicky Unruh argue for the uniqueness of Latin American Vanguardia literature in its rebellion against logic and reason.

No other era had seen such an incredible burst of new technology, thought, and science, which simultaneously brought the nations of the world closer together while at the same time thrusting them into world wars. This study will show how the initiators of the new novel in Latin America had "transgressed boundaries, potent fusions, and dangerous possibilities," notions of Postmodern theory (Haraway 154) which fits Vanguardia style surprisingly well. A less self-centered artist than his immediate Modernismo (equivalent to Parnassian/Decadent periods) predecessors or Romantic precursors, the Vanguardia artist construed his work as a form of activity in step with vigorous times, synthesizing the lyrical and the analytical into an artistically self-critical position, detached from and simultaneously critically engaged with the period in question. These novelists constructed complex and unfinished characters as central figures in their fiction to intellectually debate the modern artist's own creative paradox (Unruh 82-83).

Although some postmodern critics declare the novel dead, post mortem was never decided (Kernan 21). For others, the novel was only

born with the twentieth century. Mikhail Bakhtin, who began his
critical writing in the 1920s (although little of it was published or
translated until decades later), considered that the novel is "the sole
genre that continues to develop, that is as yet uncompleted." Other
genres, such as the epic and tragedy, have been exhausted (Bakhtin 3).
Only the novel includes, ingests, and devours other genres without
losing itself; it alone is "organically receptive" to new forms of
perception or reading. In fact, the novel would "become for the
contemporary world what the epic was for the ancient world" (10).

In his essay "Epic and the Novel," Bakhtin says that the rapid
technological change and intense activity of the new century enhanced
the novel's evolution:

> In this actively polyglot world, completely new relationships are
> established between language and its object (the real world), and this is
> fraught with enormous consequences for all the already completed
> genres that had been formed during eras of closed and deaf
> monoglossia. In contrast to other major genres, the novel emerged and
> matured precisely when intense activization of external and internal
> polyglossia was at the peak of its activity (12).

Recent theory has varying ideas as to the viability of the
contemporary novel. While Bakhtin saw the possibilities, Harold
Bloom says novels that revealed real-world (i.e., sociological or
ideological) information would be "tarnished" (Begley 34). The novels
Bloom selects to form his "Western Canon" (the title of his 1994 book)
are valued only for their esthetics. Another critic cites "Western"
thought as preventing interpretations, because the critic's interpretation
could be invented: "Can one look for structure without structuring?"
asks Trinh Minh-ha in her recent study on postcolonial writing by
women of color (141). The purpose of her book is to show that stories
do not always have a beginning, development, climax, and closure as
Western thought suggests:

> Life is not a (Western) drama of four or five acts. Sometimes it just
> drifts along; it may go on year after year without development, without
> climax, without beginnings or endings . . . . In life, we really don't
> know when an event is occurring; we think it is starting when it is
> already ending, and we don't see its in/significance" (143).

Now, is one critic right and the other wrong, or could an answer lie
between both responses? A product of Western thought, Vanguardia
narrative identifies no beginning or closure in its search of the artist's
inner depths in order to reveal artistic reality. It is unlikely Bloom

would have argued for the Vanguardia artist, whose creation does not follow the structure of Western drama or fiction. Nonetheless, early innovative prose writers have influenced contemporary Latin American novelists which Bloom *has* placed in his canon. More and more contemporary writers, like Vargas Llosa, are beginning to acknowledge the influence on them of Vanguardia narrative. The Vanguardia novelist sought to "reconstruct boundaries" (Haraway 181), much as the Postmodern artist does presently.

According to Bakhtin, all cultural production is dialogic, in continuous struggle among several voices. If a revolutionary novelist writes to supplant previous voices, is the writer ideologically countering old masters or is he/she an artist of extreme individuality? A postmodern question is: How does one create a future that will acknowledge and incorporate the past without repeating it? It is a question that concerned the Vanguardia writers. If the postmodern is a moment of extreme self-consciousness, according to Lacanian thought, so was the Vanguardia; however, its question was how to avoid the impasse of recuperation. In order to incorporate without repeating, parody and irony became essential to the dialogic Vanguardia process.

Bloom thinks the true artist must be removed from the world and its ideologies, but what of removing the artistic creation from master narrative control, in other words, resisting esthetic and traditional paradigms? The Vanguardia artist removes himself from the world, but he also defies tradition, thereby committing an ideological act. In postmodern times, this act is called a deconstruction of master European narratives or, a loosening of the bindings of the traditional novel (Spivak 263).

Marxism—at root a romantic ideology—began to appear in narrative fiction in the high age of Romanticism. It faded with the turn of the century, and emerged again in Russian theory of the 1920s, which has only recently been translated to English and applied to literature. Scientific and technological developments in the late nineteenth century led to a worship of logic which, in turn, affected myth, that is, the basis of story form. Science brought new heroes to prose fiction, such as the detective and the spy, and new subjects, such as western and science fiction. These evolutions in thought, ideology, and science led to artistic conclusions that nature and rationalized religion no longer provided a basis for meaning in prose fiction. Alvin Kernan notes in his landmark study, *The Death of Literature* (1990), that art is not a reality or definite object, but instead, whatever society says it is at any given time (31). In discussing the 1989 Mapplethorpe artistic scandal in Chicago, Kernan cites a museum director's comment that "art often deals with the extremities of the human condition" (29).

Touché for the Latin American Vanguardia novelists, who excelled in documenting social chaos and social change, in specific urban settings of the 1920s. While French deconstructionists separate the components of literary language and texts, Marxists show how narrative has been used as an instrument of power to establish ideology (Kernan 212). Either the text has no meaning, or it has scores of meanings. A literature is only new if it neither seeks lofty esthetic goals nor influences ideology. It must only exist for itself, creating its own influence. These analyses were not possible early in the century; the Vanguardia novel's intention becomes clearer in light of current theory.

If Marxism (or any ideology) did not work, and literature is unraveling as Kernan says, then we need to re-examine, reread those works overlooked by critics, from a new perspective. This is the "excentric" position, according to Postmodern theorist Linda Hutcheon. Postmodern theory does not invert, but uses the double paradox to critique the Center from both the inside and the outside. Now, in postmodern times, we perceive the Boom as the Center, thus placing the Vanguardia on the margin, much like contemporary, postmodern narrative. The Vanguardia novel wanted to be "a novel," but only if it could parody, both incorporate and challenge the novel as it had been—now defined as a postmodern trait (Hutcheon 251).

While critics largely disagree on the inception of postmodern narrative—some deciding it begins in the 1970s and others suggesting it began immediately following the Vanguardia period—there are strong arguments for the similarities between the postmodern and the Vanguardia. Jean-Francois Lyotard defines the postmodern as "incredulity" toward metanarratives, a direct product of progress in the sciences (Lyotard 72). Bakhtin says a variety of discourses on a textual space establishes a resistance to the dominance of any one (Lodge 1990, 22). And Hutcheon saw the need for modern fiction to parody master works in order to supplant them. If metanarratives are suspect, and the traditional hero, voyage, and goal of narrative is defunct in new literature, where does legitimacy reside? Lyotard observes that Postmodernism refines sensitivities to invent, to see differences, and to tolerate the incommensurable (73). Therefore, the twentieth century novel could only become new if it rebelled from tradition and master narratives, and demonstrated the way to *new* narrative.

Finally, language itself must be free from convention (a belief and action inherited from the French Cubists who wanted to liberate words). The Vanguardia novelists freed their language, setting an example that postmodern novelists would take a step further (for example, in Mexican Carmen Boullosa's novel *Llanto* (1992), words float without conventional structure). Theorist Donna Haraway states that postmodern language expresses an awareness of matter and imagination in continual interaction, and that only partial perspectives promise objective vision (190).

In Naturalism and Realism, the artist sought to reveal a reality outside the esthetic emphasis of Romanticism. As a part of Albert Einstein's generation, the Vanguardia artist also seeks a perspective that had not been revealed previously. His struggle for language (non-language) is "against perfect communication, against the one code that translates all meaning perfectly, the central dogma of phallogocentrism" (Hutcheon 175). The new novel—then and now—would be a non-novel that defied master narratives.

The novels in this study represent a variety of regional settings. However, they have in common a lack of "structure"—their own particular new creations of non-structure—and a discourse that critiques the conventional novel and shows the act of creating new fiction. Each was a first in their respective countries, for their abstract quality and outrageous defiance of traditional narrative. Each is also a highly achieved artistic creation, and a representation of specific Latin American identities. The creators of these novels were not hailed by their contemporaries nor subsequent generations. It is only today that they can be saluted for showing twentieth century narrative the future of prose fiction.

---

[i] From Roger Shattuck's landmark study on the French avant-garde, p.325.

CHAPTER TWO

MEXICO'S FIRST ANTI-NOVEL

While the roaring twenties in most metropolitan cities was an era of exciting new freedoms and economic boom, in Mexico after the 1910 Revolution, it was also a dangerous time. People were often assassinated for ideological reasons and political loyalties continually shifted. Of the two institutional powers in Mexico after independence—the church and the military—only the latter emerged stronger from the Revolution. Military infighting, however, continued to destabilize the new command. Controlling nearly one half the nation's land until the Revolution, the Catholic Church had held its stronghold for decades after independence from Spain (Skidmore 227). When the Mexican Constitution of 1917 was enacted, the church lost vast land holdings and its autonomy, empowering the government to redistribute land. Still, the Church never lost its sway over the populace, which plagued the new government through the 1920s. What began in 1910 as the overthrow of the entrenched dictator Porfirio Díaz developed into a social revolution, changing significantly the power and property relationships in Mexico. Mexico's revolution was totally modern, preceding by six months the Russian Bolshevik revolution.

The outlying destabilizing forces of Emiliano Zapata and Pancho Villa were finally overcome when they were killed in 1919 and 1923, respectively, and the first multi-year presidents were able to exert control through a central government. Their own infighting finally came to a halt in 1928 when Alvaro Obregón was killed by a religious fanatic. The fear of communism or other nonconservative political ideologies led the government to quell every perceived threat, resulting in frequent assassinations of intellectuals. In her novel *Tinísima* (1992), Mexican writer Elena Poniatowska aptly captures the paranoia and violence of the 1920s and the (real-life) assasination of Cuban communist writer Julio Antonio Mella in January 1929. Poniatowska's novel is a semi-fictionalized biography of Italian-American photographer Tina Modotti, who lived with photographer Edward Weston in Mexico City in the early 1920s. By February 1926, Weston had become tired of Mexico, disgusted with the violence and uncertainty he perceived:

> Weston se había hartado de las noticias de iglesias incendiadas, trenes volados y los ¡Viva Cristo Rey! en la calle. "Estos son lunáticos, todos los fanáticos son locos, este país es peligroso". . . . --Corren rumores de una tregua religiosa; los cristeros se han replegado, las iglesias ya no son asaltadas, los ensotanados podrán volver a su paz de los sepulcros. ---No seas ingenua, Tina, aquí todo termina mal. Las cuentas se saldrán con muerte. Estoy harto de balas y de pistoleros. A Xavier Guerrero, en cambio, le entusiasmó el cierre de las iglesias. Tina sorbió sus palabras como maná del cielo. Nada había dañado tanto al pueblo como el fanatismo religioso, los pinches curas prometen el paraíso a cambio de la esclavitud sobre la tierra: "Con el control de cultos, el país pasará de la infancia a la madurez". . .(Poniatowska 210-211).
> [Weston was fed up with the news of torched churches, derailed trains and the "Long live Christ the King!" shouts on the street. "These are lunatics, all the faithful are crazy, this country is dangerous". . . . "There are rumors of a religious truce, the Christers [Catholic militants] have calmed down, churches are no longer held up, and those in hiding should be able to return to the peace of the graves." "Don't be so naive, Tina, here everything ends badly. The bill's sum is death. I'm sick of bullets and gunmen." Xavier Guerrero on the other hand, was enthused about the closing of the churches. Tina soaked up his words like mannah from heaven. Nothing had harmed the people as much as the religious fanatiscism, the damn priests who promised paradise in exchange for slavery on the earth. "Once the cults are controlled, the nation will move from infancy to maturity".][i]

In nationalistic terms, Mexico's second decade of the century was a spiritual time. Although Mexican fought Mexican in the Revolution, the unifying goal was to overthrow a European system and create a true Mexican political autonomy. In 1921, the nation celebrated one hundred years of independence from Spain, and the new government encouraged poets to wax poetic for the glory and honor of the country. While loyalty to Mexicanness was strong, it took an entire decade for the new government to stabilize. The first long-term presidents, Alvaro Obregón (1920-24) and Plutarco Elías Calles (1924-28), were opposed by both the political right (the "cristeros") and the left (artists, intellectuals and, later, union leaders seeking to create a communist or socialist government). These administrations gained loyalty by supporting literacy programs and art projects. During the Obregón administration, writers, intellectuals, and Minister of Education José Vasconcelos undertook an ambitious rural educational campaign, designed to help Mexicans fight illiteracy and support their new government. Vasconcelos was a crusader of messianic proportions, drawing the support of the celebrated Chilean poet Gabriela Mistral (Franco 1989, 102).[ii] National theater and literary groups were created, often assisted by wealthy patrons such as Antonia Rivas Mercado (a loyal supporter of Vasconcelos). Mercado helped fund the Contemporáneos group in the late 1920s, and the first avant-garde theater (Ulysses Theater), as well as aiding the publication of books in the mid-1920s written by bohemian avant-garde writers (113). The Calles' government fought the Church's opposition to an institutional government (now controlling capital expansion), and discouraged cultural ideas outside those it directed. While the Calles administration allowed certain labor groups to create unions, it thwarted other political movements, including Vasconcelos' bid for presidency (Sefchovich 74). There was little land distribution until the late 1920s, and it was abruptly stopped by 1930.

Between 1910 and 1917, a million Mexicans died in the Revolution. Survivors found little economic opportunity, and the future of post-Revolution Mexicans was becoming tightly managed by the strongest and most victorious generals, which both aided and hindered artistic production in the 1920s. Mostly revolutionary, the new prose of the era would gain little respect because it lacked nationalistic tones. Revolutionary concepts were acceptable under government approval, such as the mural work of Diego Rivera, David Alfaro Siqueiros, and José Orozco, prominently displayed on public buildings. Popular artistic themes included nationalism, pre-Hispanic culture, the dignity of modern peasants, anticlericalism, communal efforts, and the triumph of Marxism over Capitalism.

Mixing conservative and revolutionary elements furthered economic planning, and laid the foundation for future prosperity. Although some sectors improved, annual economic growth in the 1920s was less than two percent. It was an improvement over the declining production of the Revolution years, but such slow growth was worsened by the depression of 1930. While the Revolution gave impetus to artists who sought to be the real interpreters of a new Mexican art, these artists were not necessarily involved in the Revolution, but only affected by its violence and chaos (Schneider 1975, 160).

For Mexico to prosper, it had to reject a long-entrenched philosophical and educational system of positivist thinking, associated in Mexico with the overthrown Porfirio Díaz dictatorship. The European avant-garde manifestos called for ways to display new philosophies and scientific ideas through art: Filippo Tommaso

Marinetti's 1909 manifesto on Futurism announced eleven separate statements on the esthetics of speed, machine power, the industrial revolution, and the overthrow of theory. As Futurism came to represent a glorification of aggressive and warlike sentiments, in the period following World War I, Marinetti and others allied themselves with Fascism in Italy. In Spain (and throughout Latin America), Ramón Gómez de la Serna translated and published the futurist manifesto in 1910 in his journal *Prometeo* (Leal 158). *Futurismo* was the Latin American term given to incipient avant-garde work. In Latin American cities, infused with global awareness between 1900 and 1920, this was essentially a period of transition, from its most recent Modernismo to a *Vanguardia* movement. In Mexico, the Vanguardia movement is expressed first through the Estridentistas and then the Contemporáneos.

After the 1910 Revolution (some theorists believe the Revolution continued into the 1920s), Mexican artists sought to reflect their society in transition and the rapidly changing world-at-large. To do so, they did not have to join the Communist Party, but simply attack conventional bourgeoise art. Latin American literati who had traveled to Paris after the turn of the century returned to their countries with new ideas. They advocated the overthrow of Nationalism, the literary movements of Romanticism and Realism, and the logic of Rationalism for creating art. Increased magazine and newspaper consumption in Latin America after the turn of the century heightened an awareness of these new movements. The Mexican Estridentista movement (essentially 1921-26) used poetry and manifestos to hail the Russian Revolution, express support for the Proletariat, and decry Capitalism; in fact, it is believed the Estridentista movement was a prolongation, in both literature and art, of the 1910 Revolution (González 83).

The Estridentista movement was first active in Mexico City during 1922-27 (then it relocated to Xalapa, Veracruz), and appropriated Marinetti's theories extensively (Leal 157). The movement's principal participants were Manuel Maples Arce, Luis Quintanilla, Germán List Arzubide, Arqueles Vela, and Salvador Gallardo, but it was Vela who produced a novel.*El café de nadie* (No One's Cafe; 1926), named after the cafe that the Estridentistas frequented in Mexico City, not only turned detective fiction on its head (and thus the logic of Rationalism), but also used metaphors and verbs that glorified mechanization and modernity. Poniatowska makes reference to this movement in her novel *Tinísima* (Tina Modotti was also considered an Estridentista):

20 de agosto de 1923. . . : Al salir de la cena, las calles estaban vacías. "¿No hay centros nocturnos en México? ¿Dónde está la gente?", preguntó Weston. "Están ocupados adentro", enfatizó Federico

malicioso, "pero si quieren vamos al Café de Nadie. Lo acaban de abrir los estridentistas, esos adoradores de Dadá". Manuel Maples Arce y Germán List Arzubide se levantaron a saludar a Tina. List lo hizo con una caravana: "Somos sus más rendidos admiradores". Ni siquiera le dedicó a Weston una segunda mirada. . . . (Poniatowska 143).
[August 20, 1923. . . : Upon going out after dinner, they found the streets empty. "Isn't there any night life in Mexico City? Where are the people?" Weston asked. "They're otherwise occupied indoors," Federico said maliciously, "but if you want we could go to the Café de Nadie. The Stridentists, those Dada lovers, just opened it." Manuel Maples Arce and Germán List Arzubide got up to greet Tina when they walked in. List curtsied and said: "We are your most devout admirers." But they didn't give Weston a second look . . . .]

The Estridentistas were a cohesive group, and few in number in the early years when there was competition from the social realist novel, practiced by those who wanted to document the Revolution or regionalism.The artist who sought a universal, urbanized perspective found it necessary to do something more dramatic: he rebelled against traditional form to reveal the chaos of contemporary society (as Tina Modotti attempted in her photographs or Diego Rivera in his murals). The manifestos demanded violence, and the Vanguardia artist violently attacked conventional artistic form. Although closely connected to Europe through a larger artistic feeling, the Mexicans and other Latin Americans realized that European cultural values no longer had meaning, for Europe itself was casting about wildly to find artistic stimulus in other cultures. Not only had Mexican artists discovered their own culture following the Revolution, they were now aware of their innate ability to reveal a particular Mexican subconscious.

Vela's novel accomplishes three things: (1) it creates a new, abstract form that was later adopted by the Boom novelists or their precursors such as Juan Rulfo; (2) it criticizes (using parody and irony) and seeks to supplant traditional literature and philosophy; and (3) it is the first narrative in Mexico to do so. In breaking with traditional structure, it created a dehumanized world, one that rejected sentimental, romantic responses and which would later be called "*anti*literature," not unlike Bertoldt Brecht's theater or Jean Genet's fiction:

That *anti-* is a revolution against a type of society which speaks in lies, which feigns an ethic, and which murders to survive. On a literary plane, this revolution recreates the forms of expression, naturally, but this is not what really matters, (just as the important thing in a revolution is not the dynamiting of a government palace, the Congress, and the law courts). The revolutionary artist rips out the seams of institutional art not because he must follow a certain program, but rather out of personal necessity. In the process he sees himself and judges himself. It is *his* [sic] revolution (Alegría 182).

If the Vanguardia genre seeks to defy structure, it must "rip out the seams of institutional art," an idea vaguely similar to Gayatri Spivak's theory of postmodern fiction, or "loosening the binding of the book" (262). What else could the avant-garde writer do to attract attention to his work, to go where no one has gone before (to quote a popular U.S. television show), and to explain that a new way of representing reality was necessary—something the predecessors, the Realists, had not been able to invoke? The new novelist needed to reconstruct boundaries (Hutcheon 1993, 181). This revolutionary behavior has been seen as radical or, simply, spiteful acts without a message in its violence. They were writing in reaction to the cry from Ortega y Gasset that current (1920s) artistic production was in crisis. In an issue of the 1920s journal *El universal ilustrado*, one member of the Vanguardia states what his generation attempted to do:

> Se habla de una generación de vanguardia . . . . Se dice que esta generación está en crisis . . . . Su virtud común ha sido la desconfianza, la incredulidad. Lo primero que se negaron fue la fácil solución de un programa, de un ídolo, de una falsa tradición. Nacieron en crisis y han encontrado su destino en esta crisis: una crisis crítica (Cuesta 105).
> [The talk is of a generation of *vanguardia* . . . . It is said that this generation is in crisis . . . . Its common virtue has been lack of confidence, incredulity. The first thing it denied itself was the easy solution of a program, an idol, a false tradition. They were born in crisis and have found their destiny in this crisis:a crisis of criticism.]

Jorge Cuesta explains their goals and cites the works of several members of the Contemporáneo*s* movement—a more introverted, esthetic group that corresponds to the same Vanguardia generation as the Estridentistas, but whose production begins later in the 1920s. Principal Contemporáneos were Xavier Villaurrutia, José Gorostiza, Salvador Novo and Jaime Torres Bodet, and their initial production was published in *Contemporáneos* magazine (1928-31). While these writers also wanted to revise literature, they did not defy traditional structure nor find themselves in a "crisis of criticism" as the Estridentistas did. Their great innovation can be found in symbolism, themes of death and solitude, and their preoccupation with the "self," a Freudian concept but almost counter-revolutionary in 1920s society. Salvador Novo finds that society and history are a "repetitive version of the same masquerade," and José Gorostiza holds that everything must return to primitive chaos (Franco 1967, 194). Torres Bodet confirms the sadness of man, but links it to humanness. This theme of the sadness of human beings through the common tragedy of their Mexican destiny is reflected later in the writings of Octavio Paz (196). While the Contemporáneos use Freudianism and have the Dadaist predilection to feel and imagine emotions rather than describe them, the Estridentistas were more successful in achieving new narrative technique. (Pérez Firmat chose a Contemporáneos member for his study on Vanguardia, but he might have found more innovation by selecting an Estridentista).

Like the Surrealists in 1924, the Estridentistas seek to verbalize the sounds and the actions of chaos without explaining their feelings. The French Dadaists sought freedom from conventional language in 1916—they called it liberating words—so that artistic activity might arise from spontaneity and choice (Shattuck 358). The Surrealists interpreted freedom as a psychological liberation, using shock, curious and fragmented collections, juxtapositions of usually disassociated objects, and automatic writing. Responding to these influences, the Estridentistas sought, and Mexican writer Arqueles Vela achieved, a "contentious encounter" (in the title of Vicky Unruh's book) that provided a model for subsequent novelists.

Cuesta, like Pérez Firmat, fails to cite Arqueles Vela in his examination of anti-literature, but it was Vela's Estridentista novel that laid the foundation for the others, if Cuesta's model is to be followed. Cuesta asserts that the new artist must be an individual and follow a personal calling, for personal expression belongs to man, the nation, and the era of the person from whom it emanates (107). No generation has been less patient in trampling over the dominion of the previous generation than the avant-garde writers after the turn of the century. Arqueles Vela (1899-1972) conducts his own revolution against the novel, and creates the first antinovel, a tribute Fernando Alegría attributes to later antinovelists, such as Julio Cortázar (Argentina, 1914-1984), Miguel Angel Asturias (Guatemala, 1899-1974), and Alejo Carpentier (Cuba, 1904-1980). Hence, Vela is a forerunner of the Latin American antinovel.

Mexican Vanguardia fiction is not only similar to post-1970s fiction—Vela's posthumous novel *El intransferible* (The Untransferable), published in 1977 but written in 1925-27, could easily be mistaken for contemporary Mexican fiction (Picón Garfield 206)—its style is evident in the years immediately following: José Revueltas' *El luto humano* (Human Suffering; 1943) is considered by one critic to be "the first novel written by a Mexican author in which an attempt is made to apply modern novelistic techniques" (Leal 112).

The roots of new literary style begin in the Mexican political ambience during and after the Revolution. In the early 1920s, no conflict was apparent between avant-garde technique and revolutionary politics. Within just a few years, however, freedom in technique disappeared and political commitment became a rigid requirement for artists. A new Mexico-in-the-making required a politically-committed, socio-regional novel to record its history and identity. Technique was unimportant. The Estridentistas' artistic revolution rendered their work difficult to categorize; they were criticized for lack of structure and reality. As a result, the first antinovelists went without recognition. In order to create that new, abstract novel and supplant tradition, the novelist had to examine (by citing and parodying) earlier formats and demonstrate that conventional structure does not work in the new century. Vela's novel is advice to other writers, an attempt to explain how he seeks inspiration and channels it to create art. A tool he used referenced the previous generation (the Modernistas), who, in order to demonstrate their surge of artistic inspiration and its resultant work, portrayed woman as muse and eroticism to demonstrate inspiration. While the act of creating was often represented as a *petit mort* (little death or sexual climax) by the Modernistas, the Estridentistas sought a new representation of artistic inspiration, using technological motifs, as in Vela's novel *El café de nadie.* Vela appropriated the woman-as-muse concept in order to explain his inspiration.

For the Vanguardia artist, inspiration surges from the city, the future, and from a hope for unity within the city, where deductive reasoning does not help him. Vela said his intent was "to create art for the present and not the past" (González 86). Vela lived in an age when Einstein's theories had turned the world upside down. For the first time in history, science was reinventing science, turning on itself with new theories that defied earlier reasoning. Vela brings out that awareness in his novel.

El café de nadie is a novel in three parts, in reverse order of completion:the last part, "La señorita, etc." was published in *El universal ilustrado* in 1922; the second part, "Un crímen provisional" (A Provisional Crime) was published in *El universal* in 1924; and the first part, "El café de nadie" (No one's cafe) appeared for the first time as part of the novel in book form in 1926. The order of the three parts in the book is based on the last to the first written and published, that is, "El café de nadie" is followed by "Un crímen provisional," and "La señorita, etc."

Although unconnected in plot, the three parts similarly parody a passing era to present a new vision. "La señorita, etc." is the recollection of a male character who travels by train, streetcar and on foot, always remembering his lovers, who could be several different women or the same one. In "Un crímen provisional," a detective arrives at the scene of a murder (the apartment and office of a man who is not present), and begins his analysis in Sherlock Holmes fashion; one by one, other parties arrive: a butler-type servant, a woman who worked for the missing man/suspect, and, finally, the suspect himself. "El café de nadie" is essentially the story of a cafe and its clientele, principally the only person with a name, Mabelina, and two regulars (men) who appear to never leave the cafe. The woman's thoughts are the sole plot.

Together, the three parts—novelettes or novellas—consist of the following: a tribute to Futurism in "La señorita, etc."; the demise of Rationalism by means of its own detective novel in "Un crímen provisional"; and, as a result of each, the arrival of the new Future and departure from the old logic. The first part of this novel, "El café de nadie," is a vision of creative inspiration, based on new theories, especially relativity.   Einstein's theories on Relativity say that acceleration and deceleration create no apparent difference in a line or circle; hence, narrative fiction is not hindered by either direct flow or stops and starts.

In the original edition, the first "novella" (English word for short novel, although the author called each of these a "novela" in Spanish, meaning a standard novel), is 32 pages long, the second is 23 pages, and the third is 19. Literary critics like John Brushwood call them "short stories," even though each part is separated into 10, 6 and 8 chapters, respectively. Vela was calling attention to a new, brief way of constructing the novel by insisting that each of the three parts were novels. In this study, the novels that make up *El café de nadie* will be examined in order of publication, therefore, the shortest, "La señorita, etc." is first, followed by "Un crímen provisional," and then "El café de nadie," the longest and first section in the book. They will be examined to determine influences/impact of the technological age; therefore, it is important to consider them chronologically in terms of completion.

The number of pages in each of the "novellas" shows no consistency or logic, but a search for numbers is highlighted in the novel. The Italian Futurists used numbers in disorder to demonstrate the impact of technology and science. Vela's posthumous novel, *El intransferible*, also relies on numbers, where disorder suggests a multi-presence with the concepts of one and all (a human being and the universe).   In the one-within-the-all are the notions of return, metamorphosis and transubstantiation, confirmed by a play of numbers, especially the combinations of 3 and 7 (Picon Garfield 208-209). This insistence on numbers reflects the author's predilection for the scientific spirit (especially Einstein) and exact sciences of new technological society.

Vela is considered an important member of the Futuristic movement in Mexico, and he excels for brevity in his prose; in fact, Vela emphasizes brevity. Many of his sentences are short, consisting of only two or three words; on numerous occasions every second sentence is short, as seen, for example in "La señorita, etc.":

> El sueño comenzaba a desligarme.   Sentí cansancio.   Su languidescencia doblaba sobre mis brazos con la intimidad de un abrigo, se había dormido. Era natural. Seis días de viaje incómodo, la hicieron perder su timidez. No era por nada . . . (Vela 77).
> [I was overcome by sleep. I felt tired. Her languishing form folded across my arms with the intimacy of a coat, for she had fallen asleep. It was natural. Six days of uncomfortable travel had made her lose her shyness. It wasn't for nothing . . . .]

In addition, Vela's paragraphs are repeatedly short, often only one or two sentences long. Sentences alternate between being long and short, allowing for rhythm, with short words predominating. While Vela's later work includes imaginative poetic prose and excellent metaphors, his brevity in structure is especially noticeable in this early trilogy of novels. Novels by his peers were still encumbered by long sentences and paragraphs that led to interminable realistic descriptions. In English-language literature, Ernest Hemingway's brevity in prose would bring him fame in the 1920s and 1930s and forever change fiction for North Americans. But Vela made this accomplishment several years before Hemingway published his first famous novel, *The Sun also Rises* (1926). While Vela and Hemingway were contemporaries, it is not very probable that Vela would have been aware of Hemingway's writings. (Vela did not travel to Spain until after he had written at least the early parts of *El café de nadie*. Hemingway, however, had been living in France and Spain since World War I and read Spanish.) Hence, Vela was a forerunner in rejecting old forms (long, realist images and sentences), who also attempted to adapt a new logic to narrative fiction.

In "La señorita, etc.," the third part or novella of *El café de nadie*, the short sentences and paragraphs accelerate the pace, leaving memories behind and, by returning to the city, moving toward this "señorita." The train movement produces her memory (an idea used by European stream-of-consciousness writing, and also in Futurism, to show thought process).

The narrator finds himself in "un pueblo vulgar" (a common village; 75) where a bell is ringing, near the Gulf of Mexico and six hours (although two pages later he refers to six days) from the city. The narrator, who wanted to go to the city, is following a woman: "Llegamos a un pueblo vulgar y desconocido" (we arrived in a common and unknown village; 75). They leave the train because the workers were on strike and had taken over the depot and the city (which was a village in the previous paragraph) is in total blackout. As they walk, the street passes under their feet like a cinematic projection (76). They watch the boats at high tide, and the narrator suddenly realizes that he may be there because of a mistaken address on his "bagaje ilusorio" (illusory baggage; 76). This is not his life. He is accustomed to living "detrás de una puerta o en el hueco de una ventana. Sólo. Aislado. Incomprendido" (behind a door or in the groove of a window. Alone. Isolated. Misunderstood; 77). This image also describes the Romantic or Realist novelist, cloistered and hidden away from society, (living in the country and close to nature), to write his/her novels.

The state of consciousness or thought process described by Vela's narrator is similar to James Joyce's narration in *Ulysses* (1922), a novel created in nearly the same time period. Vela's narrator continues to see "her" (likely his muse) from time to time, to better grasp the absurd reality of his thoughts. The narration vacillates between memory and physical presence. The narrator says they become closer, more intimate. He hates to leave her sleeping and flee, but he must. He reminisces; she may be the solitude he used to feel. So he does leave, alone, "hacia el lado opuesto de su mirada" (in the opposite direction of her look; 78).

The second chapter begins with a countdown, from 1 to 26. The narrator considers whether it is a clock, then states it is not possible. So he considers a bell. Both images suggest urgency, the ringing to determine time, and a need to escape from this village. He decides to return to the city with its "calles estentóreas y vociferadoras" (stentorian and vociferous streets; 79). He remembers the cafe, then the trolley car, and the waitress at the cafe with whom he wanted to continue "una conversación que nunca habíamos tenido" (a conversation we had never had; 81). Memories of "her" arrive in repetitive succession in his memory (like creative impulses, or repetitions that suggest mechanical processes) until her reflection becomes lost in the glass windows of a warehouse, creating a relativist image in which mass and energy, according to Einstein, are equivalent.

Description is based on serial images: "Sus miradas, sus sonrisas, sus palabras" (Her looks, her smiles, her words; 80); "el frío nos hacía más amigos, más íntimos, más sensibles" (the cold made us better friends, more intimate, more sensitive; 75); and he wanted to "retener sus contornos, sus miradas, sus sonrisas" (retain her contours, her expressions, her smiles; 83). Not only is repetition used to emphasize an era of machination, it also serves to recall or to reach out for something, namely, artistic inspiration. This is even more apparent in the other two novellas. As seen with the above examples, the memory and desire for "her" represents art and the desire for creation. Woman is the symbol of the *ars poetique* of the Latin American Modernista movement and represented poetic creation or the search for it. Referring to the "señorita," the narrator states: "Muchas veces la esperé con un vacío interior" (many times I waited for her, with an emptiness inside; 85). But that emptiness is not filled, even with her presence: their hearts joined "con ese temblor incesante del motor desconectado repentinamente de un anhelo de más allá" (with that incessant temblor of a motor suddenly disconnected from a lofty wish; 87). It is only when she (or her presence) "penetró, con sus pasos medidos, en el ascensor (penetrates [him], with measured steps, in the elevator; 87), that he begins to feel, to create, or to think. This image of the artist's connection with the muse, or the receiving of creative inspiration, is in direct contrast to sexual imagery used by Modernistas. Here a "she" "penetrates" *he*, the male artist.

The desire to show the motivation for inspiration and artistic creation is a trait inherited from the Modernistas, but Vela expresses a philosophy that is very different from that of the Modernistas. There is a juxtaposition of the unclear real with the illuminated unreal, and multiple layers of creative inspiration:

> Los espejos multiplicaban simultáneamente, con una realidad irrealizable de prestidigitación... En mi imaginación ya no existía solamente ella, no era solamente ella; se fundía, se confundía con esta otra ella que me encontraba de nuevo en el rincón del café (80).
> [The mirrors multiplied simultaneously, with an unrealizable reality of prestidigitation . . . In my imagination she didn't just exist by herself, it was not just her; it was fused, she was confused with this other she that came to find me again in the corner of the cafe (80).]

In chapter four, the narrator begins by stating that at the same time, every day, he boards the trolley, thereby structuring his days, eight to twelve-thirty and three to five-thirty. His muse enters his consciousness at every juncture: "she" balances harmoniously on the handlebars of the trolley. Working in an office, he seeks to reach the "intellectual" elevators (84). In section five, "la vida casi mecánica de las ciudades modernas" (the nearly mechanical life of modern cities; 87) introduces a series of verbs that indicate movement and mechanical action: "Mi voluntad ductilizada giraba en cualquier sentido" (My will spun with any feeling); "me volvía mecánico" (I became mechanical);

"Me conducían las observaciones" (I was conducted by my observations); and "yo era un reflector de revés que prolongaba las visiones exteriores" (I was a rear-view mirror that prolonged outside vision; 88). Even sexual tension is mechanical: "sus senos y mi corazón se quedaron temblando, exhaustos, con ese temblor incesante del motor desconectado repentinamente" (her breasts and my heart stayed trembling, exhausted, with that incessant sputtering of a motor that suddenly quit; 86-87).

These futurist images give the sense of an inevitability of mechanizing life and, perhaps, of a mechanical creation. The machinery has a human feel to it, and nature fuses with man's creation: "los cláxon de los automóviles olfateando la traza de los viajeros" (the honks of the automobiles sniffing the tracks of the travelers); and "el otoño comenzaba a recoger las primeras hojas volantes" (autumn began to collect the first leaflets scattered by the wind; 82). Chapter six introduces automatic piano music to his thoughts of "her," with her silhouette tattooed to the depths of his heart. She is not only a union organizer, but also a feminist—her voice has the "telephonic" sound of feminism (90)—and she tries to encourage him to make a spiritual revolution. In chapter seven he has to deceive himself in order not to seek the clarity of her shadow. He is still trying to shake himself from her "influence," but nothing works. Her steps scrape against the numerically accumulated silence in his armchair (92). Finally, the last chapter consists of four short paragraphs. After a long spiritual journey, he has discovered only that his evocations are punctured by her looks, like an ellipsis. He reviews them without thinking. Although he has felt her nearness and influence, the artist also feels frustration when a creative impulse/process eludes him. "She"—the new creation so ardently sought—feels unattainable.

This novella, novel, or third part of El café de nadie essentially describes the tumultuous inner being of the citizen of an industrial and mechanized society (González 87), but also, metafictionally, the artist seeking inspiration in the new era of the twentieth century. Vela wrote this short novel in response to the call for a new literature. His muse is not the tangible or identifiable Modernista muse, but one who is technological and modern and who moves him to thought processes that will bring about new narrative for the modern era.

The Modernistas and the French Decadents used a shapely female form and the sexual, erotic act to demonstrate their creative spirit, but Vanguardia artists would transform and mechanize this image of muse. The Latin American Vanguardistas were influenced by the 1924 Surrealism movement in Paris, where members displayed the female form in their first workplace, a large drawing room known as *La Centrale Surréaliste*:

> There was a woman in the Surrealist room—her only peculiarity being that she was not made of flesh and blood. The woman in question was a life-size reclining nude figure, a mannequin, armless and headless, suspended from the ceiling of the Centrale. Her function was evidently to inspire the "anxious men" who came there to unburden themselves of their secrets (Suleiman 21).

This text includes photographs (22-25) showing a dozen men standing around a table and the nude figure suspended above them. As "Un crímen provisional" is discussed, it will be interesting to recall this image.

Luis Buñuel and Salvador Dalí (members of the Parisian Surrealism movement) produced a short film in 1928, "Un chien andalou," which draws on the Freudian idea of repressed desires to be discovered by tapping the subsconscious. Thoughts are manifested in a profusion of free images, linked in many instances to a woman's body: her eyeball is slit in an early scene, indicating a desire to see more than is allowed by society; a man fondles her breasts, and quick edits show her clothed and then bare-breasted as though his thoughts were being revealed; and her underarm hair, in the shape of pubic hair, suddenly appears in place of his mouth. The woman is used in this film as an image suggesting release (a final scene is of the metamorphosis of a butterfly) of an inner subconscious desire or will. While the film was made a few years after Arqueles Vela wrote his three-part novel, it depicts what he was seeking—a release for subconscious desire to create new narrative. His use of mechanical metaphors and repetitions demonstrate his path toward artistic creation. Whether the Modernistas' representation of sexual climax, the Surrealists' display of a mannequin or breasts in a film, or the Estridentistas' description of penetration by a woman's memory, women were the symbol in the avant-garde era of the creative spirit desired, or a revelation of the artist's subconscious.

The title of the second novella, "Un crímen provisional," suggests relativity by provisionality. Vela's style of short phrases continues, although without repetitive descriptions, but the content of this novella is based on the analysis of a crime. The unnamed "Detective" examines a woman's cadaver in "una pose escogida por ella misma" (a pose she chose for herself; 51) and, in his initial deduction, he decides that she was not killed in that room but in another. He interrogates a nervous servant who hands him one business card after another (indicating various roles and professions—mining engineer, ambassador, lawyer, doctor—with different names). Then a woman (whose arrival takes up two pages as the detective listens to footstep sounds on the staircase, in the hallway, and near the door of the apartment) clears up matters by declaring that the business cards represent one and the same person, her employer and the servant's employer. The detective proceeds to "dissect" (57) the newly arrived woman as he questions and analyzes her. She states that her employer "es incapaz de asesinar, sin embargo, yo presencié los ensayos" (is incapable of committing murder, nevertheless, I witnessed the rehearsals; 60). The detective asks which role the employer played during the rehearsals, and she replies:

> El más atractivo. El personaje conquistador e irresistible. Elegante, galante, displicente y distraído. Usaba actitudes de aventurero romántico. Un traje claro a grandes cuadros amarillos (60).
> [The most attractive one. The conquering and irresistible character. Elegant, gallant, disagreeable and distracted. He assumed the attitude of the romantic adventurer. A light suit with large yellow checks.]

There is a moment of silence while the detective takes a drag on a Russian cigarette (a Socialist statement against Capitalism). Then he asks her if she noticed any details about the woman. She responds negatively, only that she had blubbered one word with a discolored voice. He asks why it was a discolored voice. The woman is sure the other woman's voice was discolored, distorted, insincere, unexcited, toneless. But the detective still wants to know what word she pronounced. She does not remember, adding that she simply cannot reconstruct it, but she tells him the woman seemed to speak a strange and extravagant language, or various languages. He asks if it was Esperanto. After another pause of several minutes "tan incomensurables como esos de los sueños" (as incommensurable as those in dreams; 61), the detective asks what color her voice was. The woman employee simply starts talking about hearing another person in the next room, whom she supposes was a woman. Then she says the man came into her room holding a revolver and acted out the part of an assassin. When he finished, he crossed the hall and, in the room next door, she heard a shot.

Suddenly, she and the detective hear footsteps on the stairs. She whispers that it must be him (62-63). Finally, the employer (and supposed criminal) arrives and proceeds to confess. One woman is dead, and the criminal explains that he had to kill her. The other woman helps the detective in his analysis, using the process of deductive reasoning. The muse of the past--voluptuous woman--had to be killed, and the muse (creative spirit) of the twentieth century helps the detective.

The detective states that "Este crímen no está en el catálogo de mis observaciones" (This crime is not in my catalog of experience; 53). Although he examines each room, inspecting the blinds, imagining the echo of compromising phrases and the trajectory of "pisadas criminales" (criminal footprints; 55)—along the lines of a Sherlock Holmes mystery—the detective does not fulfill the usual role of rational Anglo-Saxon fiction, on which the conventional detective novel is based. He makes no conclusive deductions. The murderer says: "Mi única defensa es el crímen" (My only defense is the crime; 65). Then he explains that when one day, "tropecé con la mujer irresistible, toda mi fuerza y todo mi anhelo se polarizó en su indiferencia y en la imposibilidad de conquistarla" (I stumbled across the irresistible woman, all of my force and all of my longing was polarized in her indifference and the impossibility of conquering her; 65).

She had remained mute in spite of everything he did. He took on different personalities, hoping to win her attention, but to no avail. Still, her eyes expressed desire for him as her ideal man (65). He worked to gain her attention, and one day he said to her: "Por tí, sería capaz de cometer un asesinato" (For you, I would be willing to kill; 66). Suddenly, she fell into his arms, "besándome frenética" (kissing me frenetically; 67). He never thought such an innocent phrase would bring her intimacy "para siempre" (forever; 67). He planned to "comprar la vida de alguien que estuviese desesperado" (buy the life of some desperate person; 67). He walked the streets day and night thinking about what could make him a criminal. He found it impossible to keep living that way; there was no hope left for him but the crime itself. Finally, he finds a woman who "la exasperó siempre por su belleza, por su gracia, por sus encantos, por su inteligencia" (always exasperated [his desired woman] because of her beauty, her grace, her enchanting ways, and her intelligence; 68), so the following scenario ensued:

Cenamos varias veces, bailamos en diferentes ocasiones, íbamos al teatro los tres, con una envidiable compaginación espiritual. Cuando ella estaba preparada sentimentalmente, voluptuosamente, para presenciar el crímen, cuando presentí que lo contemplaría con un verdadero fervor, tracé los planos del asesinato y lo ensayé como un actor perfecto en un escenario perfecto (68).
[We dined together several times, danced on several occasions, we would go to the theater all three of us, with enviable spiritual agreement. When she was sentimentally, voluptiously ready to witness the crime, when I felt that she contemplated it with true fervor, I made

plans for the murder and rehearsed it like a perfect actor in the perfect scenario.]

According to this character, it is a perfect solution for a perfect situation. In a Sherlock Holmes mystery, the criminal tries to commit the perfect crime. The former literature, and even the former muse, had to be killed off in a perfect manner, then supplanted by a new literature and a new muse—a "frenetic" muse representing the new age.

The dead woman turns out to be a mannequin (69). After the criminal is supposedly arrested, he states that the "dead woman" was created by the beauty of the woman accompanying him, the only witness to the crime. With no actual murder, the detective's pursuit becomes ridiculous. Although this aspect is not explained, the would-be criminal requests at the end that "este crímen provisional, que puede ser precursor del verdadero, quede en un absoluto silencio" (this provisional crime, which could be a precursor of the real one, may remain in absolute silence; 69).

Either the would-be criminal was rehearsing for a real crime, or the final statement has a double meaning—a trait of postmodern fiction but which began in Vanguardia discourse with a dual-charged isotope (Prada Oropeza 166). The crime here is against the detective novel, the prose of rationalistic philosophy by authors such as Arthur Conan Doyle and Edgar Allan Poe. This novel, or crime, is a precursor to another on the horizon (represented with sunset and sunrise in the first part of El café de nadie). The novelist is clearly stating that the novel must be different in the future (in order to survive, Bakhtin would say). While Ilán Stavans gives Jorge Luis Borges and other Latin Americans the credit for "revising" detectivist prose (24), Vela is actually the first to parody, criticize, and bring attention to the need for revision:

> Las fórmulas genéricas están de cabeza: hay intento de solucionar preguntas enigmáricas, pero la respuesta conclusiva nunca llega . . . . (Stavans 27).
> [The generic formulas are upside-down: there is an intent to solve enigmatic questions, but the conclusive answer never arrives. . . .]

In Vela's novel, the roles of typical characters—suspects, witnesses, and criminals—are changed and, in the process, traditional philosophy is questioned. The facts and the deductions are distorted, in a frustrating and humorous parody of conventional detective fiction. A precursor of the precursors of the Latin American Boom, Vela inverts a genre to protest conventional thought and structure; he challenges this genre, parodying it, in order to question "master" narratives, as critics note about postmodern fiction (Hutcheon 1993, 252-253). He also creates and substantiates a new, revised image of creative muse.

Vela's irony is effective for its use of humor, which Carlos Fuentes calls one of the most distinguishing traits in recreating Latin American language in the new novel (30). Whether using an attractive, ladykiller suspect in a bright, checked suit, or a detective that is too stupid to tell the difference between a dead body and a mannequin, Vela engages humor, like French avant-garde writers, as a device to alter the reader's expectations (Shattuck 172). Humor in the avant-garde era was also a deliberate mask for the boldness of the artists' innovations (178). Humor becomes a tool, like the muse, that the Vanguardia novelist uses to draw attention to the need for a new genre. Humor is also a tool for acknowledging complexity, a means of survival, and affirming life (Hutcheon 1994, 26). Just as irony comes into play because discursive communities exist, so humor reinforces existence—here the existence of a creative spirit—while exposing or subverting hegemonic ideologies.

Language and style become objects and writing acquires a function; the relationship between the creative process and the state of crisis in society, according to Roland Barthes, transforms the language through innovation and creates a style (Schulman 38). Metaphor is an essential aspect of style that separates pre-Modern from Modern novelists (Schulman 39) and is used by the Vanguardia novelist to represent change in society. Vela, much like James Joyce, uses metaphor to recreate city life that controls and directs society. Both novelists seek to describe the consciousness of modern man through metaphor, a man whose thinking and actions in urban society are different from those in the rural setting of Regionalism. When Joyce was in the process of writing *Ulysses* (1922), he researched London's city directory and maps, studied city newspapers for a specific day in June, and "bombarded" friends and relatives for first-hand information about the city (Beja 65). Joyce also sought to adapt the process of consciousness to his writing, or "unspoken, unacted thoughts of people in the way they occur" (66), now identified as stream-of-consciousness writing but then still an unexplained style. Vela, likewise, seeks to identify man's state of consciousness, even inactive thought, through the routine of streetcars, trains, clocks, and office work.

Vela's three novellas reflect various states of consciousness, all taking place in a cosmopolitan life with access to modern technology. In "La señorita, etc." the narrator tries to remove himself from the city and get outside his thinking, but his thoughts always transport him back. In "Un crímen provisional," the man who has no choice but to become an assassin lives in a city: he goes to tea, out to dinner, dancing, and to the theater. On his "American"-style desk (Vela 51) he has brochures for transcontinental train service along with letterhead stationery with various professional names (like the business cards); there is electricity in his office/apartment (54); the detective carries a flashlight; the woman who arrives asks the detective if he is the "businessman" expected by her employer (58); and she was employed in response to a job advertisement. "El café de nadie" takes place in a cafe where patrons flee from the din of the city. The narrator's state of consciousness in *Ulysses* spans one day, while it attempts to comprehend life and the artistic process. Vela's narrators also examine an ambiguous world and the state of twentieth century urban life for an artist in Mexico, who must supersede previous generations and reveal the artist's subconscious. Many years later, Julio Cortázar would attempt a similar endeavor in *Rayuela* (1963; *Hopscotch*, 1968).

The first part of Vela's tripartite novel is undoubtedly important as it carries the title of the novel itself. It contains a description of the cafe where the Estridentista members met, and an enigmatic woman whose name is Mabelina. This first novel or section of Vela's book concludes by focusing on her:

> Mabelina se queda un momento indecisa. Después, rectificándose, empuja la puerta del Café hacia el alba que va levantando el panorama de la ciudad (42).
> [Mabelina hesitates indecisively for a moment. Then, rectifying herself, she pushes the door, exiting toward the dawn that is raising the panorama of the city.]

With the exception of the regulars who occupy the booth she desires, Mabelina is the principal character of this novella, but no one seems to notice her. When she walks into the cafe, she looks at the numbers on the booths or tables, seeking "la cifra exacta" (the right number). Although her companion suggests several possibilities, she chooses a booth "que tiene un poco borroso el número. Así no lo sabremos nunca" (where the number is a little fuzzy. That way we'll never know it; 17). This suggests that the logic of rational observation does not work, for there are things one can never know. It is better to choose one's own space, which may be fuzzy, but original.

In 1905, Einstein first declared that no absolute movement exists, and that no one object can be an absolute or a static reference in comparison to space. When two cafe regulars enter, one after the other, the narrator says they seem to be joined in their movements as they walk. The first to enter "adelanta el pie izquierdo, retrocediéndolo inmediatamente con el sentido mecánico de una equivocación subconciente, cerciorándose de que no es con ese pie con el que debe entrar" (puts his left foot foward, pulling it back immediately with the mechanical sense of a subconscious mistake, making sure that it is not with that foot that one should enter; 14).

Once in their booth, they do not seem to move for hours or even days. In fact, the cafe itself is a static place, where the waiter must be called repeatedly (12). Within the cafe walls is a "sound" of either sunrise or sunset (11), and thoughts that are never exteriorized drop from the electrical current (12). The "parked clocks" provide comments on the lives of the clients. While other couples, in vague hugs, come and go from other booths intermittently, the pair of regulars (for whom the door opens automatically) remain hidden in the booth's half-light of their sensations (13), and waiters remove the crumbs of impatience and napkins stained by flirting and incongruent phrases from the tables (14).

The first two chapters of "El café de nadie" document the Estridentistas' sojourn in the cafe. They are always trying to resolve the clues to their mechanical being, "nailing" themselves into their seats (15). Before speaking, one of the customers positions himself in a specific pose and straightens his suit and buttons, certain that if he were in the wrong place or untidy, he would not be able to articulate a single word (15). The other looks entirely unkempt, like a perpendicular line that has not yet been able to stabilize in its final trajectory, as if destiny had not provided him any balance (15). He walks with an air of never having touched the ground and yet he exudes the anxiety of wanting to touch and feel it (16). The two regulars are opposites, but they are connected and, as the hours go by, remain cast aside in their corner.

In chapter three, Mabelina enters for the first time and begins to search for her booth. She wants the booth that belongs to the two regulars and assumes it should be empty at this hour. But she learns that they arrive at this hour when no one else frequents the cafe (17). She leaves and with her companion walks along the avenue "ambushed" by lights (18); the streets seem to continue endlessly, similar to her thoughts that were stretching on forever. Unspoken words leave circles of silence (18). She suddenly returns to the cafe and simply stands in the darkness, staring toward the booth she wants and into the water of the mirrors. The coldness of the cafe helps her discover the impenetrable night (20). Sensing that life was over, that she had lived a parenthesis, she leaves hurriedly.

Chapter Four begins at the hour lights are turned on in each booth, which is when the two regulars "abandon" the cafe, and the waiters, who appear dead during the day, become electrified. Mabelina sits at the closest booth, but the furthest from her life (20). Since she can be what she is in any booth, she chooses one indiscriminately. She thinks about her first meeting with "him," how he excluded himself from life and everyone, even himself, in the streets, in conversations, at dances, and in parlor rooms. She reminisces, remembering the first time they made love, while ultraviolet rays separated her spirit from her body and flashed off and on, as in her booth (22-23). The next chapter includes some dialogue, and culminates in their first visit to the cafe, while the sixth chapter continues a conversation they hold in the cafe. This conversation was desired by the narrator of "La señorita, etc." who has frequent thoughts of "her." Chapter seven begins with the following conversation:

Eres tú . . . ?
--Casi.
--Cómo casi?
--En este momento estoy escribiendo un artículo en el que no hay sino una tercera parte de mis conceptos, de mis ideas. Un artículo que desvía esa trayectoria reincidente de mi manera de ser. Después de escribirlo no sé si, en realidad, sea el mismo de ayer. Soy un individuo que se está renovando siempre. Un individuo al que no podrás estabilizar nunca. Un individuo al que engañarás diariamente conmigo mismo por esa mutabilidad en que vivo. Cada día besas en mí a un hombre diferente (28).
[Is it you . . .?
Almost.
What do you mean *almost*?
At this moment I am writing an article in which there is only the third part of my concepts, of my ideas. An article that derails that trajectory relapsing to my way of being. After writing it I don't know if, actually, it might be yesterday's. I am an individual who is always renewing. An individual that you could never stabilize. An individual you will deceive with me myself because of that mutability in which I live. Each day you kiss a different man in me.]

The male character's loss of identity is a principal focus of this novel, much like in Luigi Pirandello's theater earlier in the century (Prada Oropeza 174). In "La señorita, etc.," the character-narrator seeks and finds a woman, seemingly a different person in each chapter, in several unusual and disconnected places (an unknown city on the gulf, a cafe, a train cabin, a streetcar, a room). The woman (or several lovers) is always referred to as "she," and she is always leaving him with an empty feeling. In "Un crímen provisional," one woman is an employee, one is the femme fatale, and a third is murdered, but she turns out to be a mannequin, inspired by the second, while the detective is set up by the first. Throughout this confusion, the assassin-to-be's identity is never clearly established. Finally, there is Mabelina, the only woman of "El café de nadie," who leaves the cafe, in the final chapter, at dawn. First, however, the regulars return to the cafe while the waiters argue over who cleans up. New tablecloths are spread and shades are pulled to shield the customers from curious glances. The regulars talk to each other about how their corner of the cafe needs no cleaning, then one of them refers to "aquella mujer que se nos queda mirando" (that woman who keeps staring at us). In her, he has found "un 50 porciento de la verdadera mujer que buscamos" (a 50 percent of the real woman we're looking for; 35). They must find the other half, they say, introduce them and, as they become close friends, these women will begin to live with the same emotions and tastes. When they become one, that one being will be theirs (35). The woman, as muse or inspiration, becomes linked to their own identities.

As they continue talking about women, one states impertinently that touching women's breasts makes them ring like bells. But that type of woman does not go to that cafe. These customers note that they are essentially the owners of the cafe, for they are the only ones who understand the place (36). The next chapter begins with a list of names--participants of the Estridentista movement. Mabelina is reading the list of names from the cafe wall, then looks in the mirror, trying to remember past lovers (suggesting she has been a lover/muse with each of them). She remembers she felt like a different person with each. But now she was regressing to the beginning of her life, where she is illiterate in emotions and sensations. It had become impossible to recuperate the series of personalities that made her (38). Feeling like a "mujer vaciada" (an emptied woman), she turns her thoughts on and off like a lightswitch to find she can reconstruct everything, yet there is no "transfusión luminosa" (luminous transfusion). Now even the muse is used up: She was turned off, lost, swaddled in the diffusion of insomnia in which she lived (39). The artist grasps for her spirit.

The final chapter of this novella opens graphically with a name Mabelina printed five times floating above the first paragraph. Each word is distinct, with extra space between the letters. In the first paragraph the reader learns she is repeatedly writing her name on the table in her booth—the letters seem to extend horizontally, stretched by her thoughts (40). As she hears her name spoken so many times, it begins to lose its meaning and the sounds become distorted and muffled. She mulls over her identity, now confused by her liaisons with men. Seemingly another person, she anxiously applies pressure on the electric button, wanting to call reality (41). She pushes the buzzer repeatedly in her booth, each time hearing the bell further and further away, as though distances were fleeing and losing themselves beyond the four cardinal points of the unreachable (42). (The four cardinal directions are also suggested by the two regulars; the woman who is fifty percent of what they are looking for; and the remaining fifty percent of woman they seek. Using a symbology of the four cardinal directions is particularly relevant to the Americas and indigenous culture, and not a focus of European art.) Finally in this novella, Mabelina snaps her purse shut as though closing her thoughts within it, and slowly walks out of the cafe.

Einstein's theories on relativity state that a ray of light from a distant star can, when passing near the sun, seem to be attracted to the mass of the sun and reflect the sun's own light. Mass and energy, according to Einstein, have equal value. But that mass has to act, that is, go toward the light or the sun's radiation. Although she confronts the "dawn" (42) of a new day, or a new future, Mabelina "abandons" and wants to "forget" her thoughts and memories of the cafe. A bell keeps ringing in the distance. The mechanical bell summons the muse, and she leaves the place where members listened to the manifestos and had gathered to create the new Estridentista movement. Now, in order to create one must abandon, even leave behind the over-used Modernista muse (not only is the Modernista era over, but the curtain is going down on the first wave of Vanguardia). This part of the novel was published in 1926. The next year the Estridentistas moved to Xalapa, a provincial town albeit university (intellectual) capital. Change was in the air; it was time to move from the first radical and violent artistic stage to the next. Mabelina, like Einstein's ray of light, retreats from what is known and moves toward light and inevitability—a fascinating explanation of changes in art upon reaching the light of artistic inspiration.

Vela wanted to demonstrate that artistic knowledge needs to move toward the sun or a new center of inspiration. To move there, however, one must leave everything behind and take great risk. The women in these three novellas represent the same illusory inspiration and artistic possibility—and frustration—that the novelist seeks and finds in mechanical, continuous movement toward the dawn of the future. The artist does not look back, but perhaps hesitates for a moment (as Mabelina does at the door before exiting), moving, changing, evolving, like life and society.

The French Cubists held that tradition had to be destroyed, and only new creations were valid. Fifteen years later, in 1931, the Chilean Vicente Huidobro showed that even new forms being imitated must be destroyed in order to return to an embryonic artistic state. He represented this idea with the use of only vowels in his master work *Altazor*. The symbolism throughout the poem refers continuously to birth and death until a final death occurs by drowning in which the poet blubbers *ai a i ai a i i i o ia* –a feeling that everything is over, and yet surprise and curiosity about what may now be possible. Huidobro's verses are traditional at first, then begin unraveling into total chaos in the poem, resulting in nothing or the beginning of something totally new—a new way of organizing language with vowels. Several years earlier, in 1926, Vela had already captured the frustration and inspiration of creativity in prose fiction by providing a three-part "novel" in which nothing ever happens—unless his revolutionary structure is considered.

Vela's short novels show the natural movement of mass as described by new scientific theory, be it the evolving of life or artistic creation. His text destroys the coherence of Realism/Naturalism based on logic and causality, similar to the artistic absurd in Antonin Artaud's 1938 anti-theater or Ionesco's absurdist plays, which begin in the 1930s. The creation of an absurd system founds its own logic (Prada Oropeza 175). Vela, James Joyce, and other novelists of the early 1920s created new artistic logic. Joyce's *Ulysses* and Vela's *El café de nadie* are each the result of powerfully dialogical imaginations. According to Paul de Man's "principle of radical otherness" (Kershner 18), dialogism sustains all voices in one, or one in all, as seen in both Joyce's and Vela's novels. These relationships between the narrator and the characters' speech, or thought, have the force to compete with the narrator's voice (and have discussions, as can be seen in Pablo Palacio's novel), which is similar to the Bakhtinian concept of double-voiced discourse, or discourse oriented toward the discourse of another (19). If these women-as-muses represent the artist's thought processes for the inception of creativity, Vela's novel demonstrates a new logic.

Vela speaks to his generation and Mexican artists of the 1920s. According to Bakhtin, the formation of the self and search for identity is a linguistic process. Consciousness is the self-articulation of an inner monologue that depends on and responds to its environment, i.e., other speech acts. Joyce gives the most scrupulous attention to intonation, accent, and gesture, during the one-day monologues of his character. Vela exacts a similar evocation in his novel, with attention given to sight and sound that portray inner consciousness.

The end of "La señorita, etc.," that is, the end of the novel, also ends the artistic search:

> Sentado al borde del crepúsculo, las repasaba sin pensar. Había peregrinado mucho para encontrar la mujer que una tarde me despertó hacia un sueño. Y hasta ahora se me revelaba. Presentía sus miradas, etc. . . sus sonrisas, etc. . . sus caricias, etc. . . . . Estaba formada de todas ellas. . . . [ellipses are author's] Compleja de simplicidad, clara de imprecisa, inviolable de tanta violabilidad (93).

[Seated at the border of twilight, I reviewed her expressions without thinking. I had traveled far to find the woman who one afternoon awakened me toward a dream. And only now was she being revealed to me. I felt her expressions, etc., her smiles, etc., her caresses, etc. . . . She was formed of all of them. Complex with simplicity, clear of impreciseness, inviolable of so much violability.]

The search ends at twilight, with an understanding that the diverse parts form a whole being. Those new inspirations, ideas, and theories must coalesce to form a new logic.

According to Vela, like Einstein, straight lines become large, continuous circles, with no beginning and no end. Vela's novel does not have an ending, and its first part was written last. The writer considers that he has not figured out anything at the end of "La señorita, etc."; the detective does nothing (no rational deduction) at the end of "Un crímen provisional"; and nothing at all seems to happen in "El café de nadie." But on the last page of "El café de nadie," Mabelina-the-used-up-muse departs, and the writer comprehends that life, and the creative act, is "formed of all" these things, unclear as they may be. For the artist, that is science.

It is only by disposing of traditional logic that new discoveries can be understood, thereby creating and resulting in a new era, based on new logic or understanding. In the 1920s, literature vacillates between two opposites (like the two regulars in the cafe), both necessary to the process of renovation in Latin America: the urban avant-garde, and Regionalism seeking to reaffirm nationalistic values in each country (Osorio 57). While contrary to each other, they fuse to become precursors of the mid-century Latin American Boom novel.

Vela's Estridentista novel is Mexico's first antinovel. Using Gayatri Spivak's imagery, Vela loosens the seams of the conventional novel, subverts structure and supplants a conventional muse. His mechanism is conceptual humor and the construction of two levels, for the reader, of isotopic discourse. The result is more than anthropomorphization but a true conceptual rupture or a surprising distortion (Prada Oropeza 166). The Vanguardistas' purpose was not to express violence and destruction, but to renovate, to give new life and form to narrative fiction. Essentially, this process is what the Boom generation is noted for, yet new connections were already being established during the Vanguardia period:

El auge de la "nueva narrativa" (la llamada narrativa del *boom*) desde los años sesenta hasta hoy, se ha estudiado como la manifestación de una producción que no se conecta a ninguna tradición, como si hubiera florecido espontáneamente. Un estudio de la prosa vanguardista deberá

describir esa tradición sin la cual no se puede entender el crecimiento
de la narrativa hispánica contemporánea (Burgos 13-14).
[The surge of "new narrative" (the narrative of the Boom) from the
sixties to today, has been studied as a display of production not
connected to any tradition, as though it had flowered spontaneously. A
study of vanguardist prose should uncover that tradition without which
the growth of contemporary Hispanic narrative cannot be understood.]

Boom novelist Julio Cortázar attempts to re-evaluate possible
influences on his generation in an article in 1970, defending the radical
nature of Boom literature and its creative process. Not surprisingly,
these beautiful words on creativity are easily applied to the
Vanguardistas:

¡Qué es un estilo, para usar una palabra ya fuera de moda, esa manera
de decir las cosas que distingue al verdadero escritor de los demás?
¿La correción, la claridad, la riqueza del vocabulario?   Basta de
bromas.   Un estilo es a la vez un imán y un espejo, es ese milagro
verbal que ni siquiera el creador puede explicar, por el cual las frases,
los períodos, los capítulos y al fin la obra entera actúan como
catalizadores de profundas y múltiples potencias; es ese don de decir
que a Pedro le duele la cabeza y decirlo de una manera que
simultáneamente abre en el lector una cantidad de caminos que llevan
mucho mas allá de Pedro y de la jaqueca . . . ¿Y todo eso es posible sin
una realidad? . . . (Cortázar 49).
[What is style, to use a word now out of style, that way of saying things
that distinguishes the true writer from others? The corrections, the
clarity, the richness in vocabulary?   Enough joking. Style is at once a
magnet and a mirror, it is that verbal miracle that even the creator
cannot explain, by which the phrases, periods, chapters and finally the
work itself act as catalysts of deep and multiple powers; it is that ability
of stating that Pedro's head hurts and saying it in such a manner that it
simultaneously opens in the reader's mind an infinite amount of paths
that lead much further than Pedro's migraine . . . And all of this is
possible without a reality? . . . (Cortázar 49).]

In *El café de nadie*, having created a new abstract form that
criticizes traditional literature and conventional philosophy, Arqueles
Vela has produced one of the first antinovels in Latin America. Critics
may not have responded favorably because of perceived
errors—stating, for example, that a train ride is first six hours and then
six days from Mexico City, and changing a village to a city within one
paragraph, in "La señorita, etc." But this was Vela's anti-methodology.
He sought no esthetic goal; but attempted, in three different examples,
to show the inspiration or first steps to artistic creation. Of the
Estridentistas and Contemporáneos during the Mexican Vanguardia

period, Arqueles Vela, an Estridentista, is the first to create a truly innovative novel and publish it in 1926, accomplishing the same as his counterpart James Joyce did for the novel in English.

---

[i] Unless otherwise indicated (as in Chapter Five) all translations of citations from the novels in this study are my own.

[ii] Vasconcelos' term ended in 1925 with his confident belief that the masses were partaking in the goods of a new, modern Mexico; although he ran for president in 1929, he soon fled the country because of threats upon his life.

CHAPTER THREE

THE MADNESS OF THE
NEW ARGENTINIAN NOVEL

Although large and wealthy in resources, Argentina suffered wars with bordering countries, dictatorships, and revolutions for most of its first century of independence. In the last two decades of the nineteenth century, however, the southern cone nation stabilized politically, prospered economically, and sprang to international recognition. It remained neutral during World War I, played a major role as a supplier of foodstuffs (primarily meat and grain) to the Allies in Europe, and began to figure prominently in hemispheric affairs, even helping to mediate a serious dispute between Mexico and the United States in 1914. By 1920 Argentina emerged as one of the leading nations of South America for its natural resources, influential landowners, and English investment in railroads, docks, packing houses, shipping and banking. Labor was scarce, but it began to arrive in droves from southern Europe (especially Italy); between 1857 and 1930 immigration to Argentina approached 3.5 million, or about 60 percent of the increase in the total population (Skidmore 74).

But prosperity created an underlying tension: By 1914, about 30 percent of the population was foreign-born, causing an Argentine confusion about its national identity. Early in the century, Florencio Sánchez (1875-1910) brought this concern to life in his realist play, *La gringa* (1904), where he showed the struggle between the Argentinian *gaucho* (Creole race) and the "gringa" (the newly-arrived immigrant from Europe).

Worldwide economic prosperity at the turn of the century produced sharp fluctuations abroad and severe repercussions at home. When its economy crashed in 1929, Argentina entered the Great Depression along with many other countries, and an influx of wealth in exports, immigrant work, and modern technology took a toll on the Argentine populace. Workers moved to cosmopolitan areas in search of jobs and a better life, but factories began to shut down. Having workers in limbo and huge gaps in income between menial workers and the aristocratic elite caused tensions. Anarchists organized against the privileged classes, but only angered the oligarchy and a rising middle class. Nevertheless, urban protest stimulated an increasing electorate (Skidmore 76). Between the increasing immigration, new prosperity and then economic depression, came the exciting decade of the 1920s, when Buenos Aires' high society enjoyed literary and arts *soirées*, with special guests from Europe. Swiss conductor Ernest Ansermet arrived in Buenos Aires in 1924, fresh from conducting the Ballets Russes in Europe, to conduct the maiden performances of a newly formed orchestra. He returned the following year and met regularly with intellectual and society dame Victoria Ocampo (years before her debut of the reknown *Sur* literary review), to discuss poetry, religion, modern music, and the people he knew, such as Stravinsky, Debussy, Diaghilev, Nijinsky, and Cocteau (Owen Steiner 67). His avant-garde music had a strong influence on intellectual society. Ocampo also hosted Rabindranath Tagore, an Indian poet who won the Nobel Prize for Literature in 1913, and was almost a cult figure, his poetry having been translated to Spanish and providing one of Spanish-speakers first contact with India (63). José Ortega y Gasset had visited Buenos Aires in 1916, also making an impact on Argentine writers.

Argentines were as educated and informed as the Europeans or North Americans; the literacy rate and a strong electorate especially increased in the early decades. Along with European immigration and international trade came news of the experimental artistic movements in France, the socio-literary awareness caused by the Russian Revolution, and the German expressionist novel. The latter's goal to reflect an interior reality (as opposed to an exterior reaction to reality through Impressionism) merged with the anguish of the Argentine economic crisis by the end of the 1920s (Schwartz 407). Sigmund Freud's *The Interpretation of Dreams* (1900) had a profound impact on the European avant-garde movements, especially Surrealism; taking note, Latin American artists expressed their feelings more strongly through distortion, jarring colors, and exaggerated linear rhythms.

Enrique Larreta's (1875-1961) novel *La gloria de don Ramiro* (Don Ramiro's Glory; 1908) attracted international attention as the first "esthetist" or decadent novel in Argentina. Although it reveals little of the inner crises that affect its antihero, it is considered an early psychological novel; set in sixteenth century Spain, it is the first twentieth century Latin American novel to explore man's failure in his search for meaning (Lindstrom 27). Later, the transition from rural life to an urban-based society highlighted the values of Argentine society and contributed to economic and societal crises that fiction writers sought to document. World War I, a dependence on an international economy, and an avalanche of new scientific discoveries precipitated an awareness of the creative spirit amid crisis.

In the first two decades of the twentieth century, Argentina's prose did not reflect any one literary school or movement, but rather many influences. As technology brought change to society, narrative fiction became more subjective. Foreign capital, aristocratic power, and tormented cosmopolitan life became the evils that were depicted in literature. Buenos Aires in the 1920s was like Chicago of the same era, a chic city flaunting its corruption (Leland 26). While poets and prose writers experimented with new ideas to find ways to explain modernization, they became polarized by an urban-rural struggle, as in many other parts of the world. Early on, leaders of two Latin American avant-garde movements, Creacionismo and Ultraísmo, launched manifestos in Buenos Aires, moving artists to seek a new Argentinian literature. Creacionismo was essentially the individual invention of the Chilean writer Vicente Huidobro (1893-1948). Based on his experiences in Europe, he presented a lecture in 1916 on Creacionismo's theory and formulaic. He was first labeled a *Creacionista* when he declared that the principal three conditions of the poet were to create, to create, and to create (Schwartz 66). Considering the artist godlike, Huidobro rejected any previous creation or convention, and sought absolute originality. While his poetry had an early impact on many Latin American poets, by the late 1920s he had moved away from his fervency for Creacionismo and, in the 1930s, he turned to writing traditional prose fiction and became involved in political activities.

Also impacting Argentine writers was the advent of Ultraísmo, promoted by Jorge Luis Borges (1899-1986) in his 1921 manifesto. Ultraísmo originated in Spain shortly after the end of World War I but in many ways, it was a combination of several avant-garde movements in France. In Spain, it ceased with the demise of the journal *Ultra* in Madrid in 1922. The movement sought to reject the outmoded Hispanic Modernismo with a more universal, rather than personal, esthetic, and it caught on quickly in Argentina after the publication of Borges' manifesto and the appearance of the journal *Prisma* that same year. Argentine Ultraísmo came to an end in 1927, when one of its proponents, Ricardo Güiraldes (1886-1927) died in Paris, after which writers moved to other political and artistic inclinations. Güiraldes is best known for his nostalgic depiction of the idealistic life of the *gauchos* in his esthetic novel *Don Segundo Sombra* (1926). This novel's rapid rise to the status of a contemporary classic reflected a need to reconcile the disturbing conflicts caused by aggressive campaigns to civilize the pampa, and to create a modern text granting ample interpretive freedom to the reader (Lindstrom 75).

In the meantime, literary circles in Buenos Aires essentially divided into two groups: the "Boedo" and the "Florida." The latter espoused an avant-garde esthetic in the journals *Prisma* (1921-22), produced as a broadside to be pasted on fences and walls; and *Proa* (1923-26), conceived as a journal of literary innovation. The members of the Florida group were first called *Ultraístas* and later *Martinfierristas* after their most important journal, *Martín Fierro* (1924-27), which included early manifestos. The name Florida came from an elegant, commercial street in downtown Buenos Aires where they would meet.

The other side of the Vanguardia "tension," the Boedo group, was led by writers such as Roberto Arlt (1900-1942). These artists were much more concerned with social and political questions, taking inspiration from the profound changes brought about by the Russian Revolution of 1917 (Forster 39). This group was named for a street in a working-class district of Buenos Aires, and their important journals were *Los Pensadores* (1922) and *Claridad* (1926-41). This group's efforts were consistently in opposition to the Florida group (although some writers were involved in both groups), but the dispute delineated differences in Argentine goals for a new literary esthetics. The Florida group sought expressive language and the Boedo group sought social change first—especially in labor and the workplace—with modifications in language as a secondary pursuit (Lindstrom 61).

From this polemic, Borges and Arlt emerged as influential Argentine writers. On the one hand, although Borges attempted to reveal the absurdity and chaos of the modern world in his short stories, his concern was primarily on esthetics. Arlt, on the other hand, wrote social satire. Like Horacio Quiroga (Uruguay, 1878-1937), Borges and Arlt embarked on an exploration of the subconscious, contributing to what is called fantasy in Latin American literature, and the creation of Magical Realism later on. Arlt used fantasy as a weapon to condemn modern society, while Borges was more concerned with philosophical and metaphysical constructions (Franco 1969, 302). Although they were peers, Borges did not produce a novel and his major short stories did not appear until the 1940s, making Roberto Arlt the lone Argentine forerunner of new narrative.

Another Argentine writer who contributed numerous manifestos to the journal *Martín Fierro* and participated in the Florida group is Macedonio Fernández (1874-1952). His work does not always figure with the other early writers, although he was considered along with Ricardo Güiraldes, the "tribal elders" of the avantgardists (Lindstrom

66). He was an innovative prose writer, who participated with the other vanguardistas in public derision of Modernismo, and especially of the writings of Leopoldo Lugones, a principal Argentinian Modernista poet. Fernández has been cited by both Borges and Julio Cortázar as a strong influence on their writing, but he was curiously unconcerned with the publication or even the preservation of his writing. It was his fellow vanguardistas who published his 1928 novel, *No toda es vigilia la de los ojos abiertos* (Not all having your eyes open is being awake), a book that seems a run-on philosophical essay with imaginative writing, and his 1929 *Papeles de recienvenido* (A newcomer's notes), of miscellaneous prose (76). The best illustration of his ideas is his *Museo de la novela de la Eterna* (Museum of the novel of the eternal woman), which, although written in the late 1920s, was only published posthumously in 1967. Half this work consists of 52 prologues (which take up 126 of the total 265 pages), followed by 20 chapters which never seem to advance the narration (Bustos Fernández 38). This book is filled with "meditations on the nature of novelistic art and language and the respective roles of writers and readers;" in fact, he spoke of making the city of Buenos Aires the setting for a fictional narrative whose readers would be required to be the characters (Lindstrom 77). While Macedonio Fernández wrote in the same time period as Roberto Arlt, his publication is more reluctant, and is only recently being re-read and studied. Many would categorize his work as equal to Arlt's as a forerunner. Although Vicky Unruh does not cite Macedonio Fernández in her text on the Vanguardia, a recent book by María Bustos Fernández (*Vanguardia y renovación en la narrativa latinoamericana*, 1996) devotes one chapter of three examples (in Mexico, Colombia and Argentina) of Latin American Vanguardia narrative to Macedonio Fernández, and I would refer the reader to this text. Her book is a great addition to new criticism on Latin American early-century literary innovation. However, the authors or works she chooses to discuss are published late in the 1920s, and therefore do not fit my scheme of earliest innovation.

In his book on the Hispanic Vanguardia novel, Gustavo Pérez Firmat does not cite Arlt as the Argentine example of Vanguardia, but rather, focuses on Eduardo Mallea (1903-1982) and his first book, *Cuentos para una inglesa desesperada* (Stories for a Desperate Englishwoman; 1926). While this text is innovative in demonstrating early Existentialist traits (Martin Heidegger only began publishing his existentialist philosophy in Germany in 1923), subsequent novels by Mallea did not appear until the late 1930s. In Spain, this novel was considered an excellent example of modernity, or new prose, but was also thought to imitate Spain's Vanguardia narrative, especially since

Mallea had written reviews of Spanish novels published in the 1920s (Pérez Firmat 14-15). Mallea's novel was indeed one of the first in Argentina to break away from Realism and Naturalism, but his novel and those by the Mexican Contemporáneos were light, humorous, with a "sunny outlook on life" (21) and impacted very little on subsequent prose fiction. However, his work was the leading representation of Latin America for many years:

> During the period that Borges was just winning notice as a short story writer, the late 1930s and 1940s, the leading figure in Spanish American literature was Eduardo Mallea, who worked alternately in the essay and the novel. Though his fame has dimmed with unusual rapidity over succeeding decades, in his prime Mallea was influential enough to set the issues for discussion in Argentine intellectual life . . .During the 1930s and 1940s he was awarded a number of literary prizes and saw his work widely translated (Lindstrom 95).

Mallea, who was Arlt's contemporary, was the editor of the highly influential literary supplement of the newspaper *La Nación*, for many years. David William Foster states, "as to Mallea, we might also suspect that at least the initial awareness of his works could be attributed to his reputation as an essayist concerned with the increasingly apparent failure in the thirties and forties of Argentine economic and social institutions" (47). Several decades later, even Borges seemed to think little of Mallea's contribution to the Argentine literary world.[i]

While Guiraldes, Borges, and Mallea were seeking to breathe new life into Argentine prose, Arlt (like Arqueles Vela in Mexico) broke radically with traditional form through subversion and parody. Mallea's "sunny" novel is quite different from Arlt's second novel *Los siete locos* (1929; *The Seven Madmen*, 1984). Arlt not only changed narrative structure and strategy, but also produced a discourse on artistic pursuit. Curiously, only since the 1970s have critics begun to study his influence on contemporary literature; for example, Foster included Roberto Arlt as a forerunner with Eduardo Mallea, Ernesto Sábato (1911-), and Julio Cortázar (1914-1984) in his study *Currents in the Contemporary Argentine Novel* (1975). Arlt sought to express the experience of life in an alienated society by creating a chaotic but artistic text. Arlt's expressionistic milieu—grimy eateries, brothels, bars and their customers—stand out in his narrative, but it is his novel's structure that marks him as an innovator. In fact, his "fragmentary, disjointed presentation and difficult-to-specify narrative data are features that later distinguish the Spanish American new narrative of the boom years" (Lindstrom 79).

Although Jean Franco separates Arlt's literary fantasy and social satire from Borges' metaphysical/philosophical fantasy, Foster believes Arlt's concern with the human dilemma to be more metaphysical than political, stemming from naturalistic, expressionistic, and existentialist roots. Arlt focuses on the alienation of technology and twentieth century society in his novel. The protagonist of *Los siete locos*, Erdosain, is a madman, but his madness is neither political nor eccentric; instead, it is a complex human reaction to a crazy world. Arlt's peers failed to recognize this accomplishment (Foster 38). A forerunner of many European novelists, according to Franco, Arlt is a pioneer at conveying personal nightmare in a world in which modern urban life is the enemy. The narrator is an anarchist who believes a return to a simpler, rural society is the only effective solution, and the solitude of nature will help man regain a sense of identity (Franco 1969, 304-305). The overt political message of Arlt's novel is the condemnation of fanaticism, be it political or religious.

The search for meaning and truth demanded new rules and required higher stakes in the modern era. William Barrett argues that "authentic" writers can find this truth with the help of their fantasies when situated at the precarious border between fantasy and insanity (87). Since the neurotic or psychotic perception of reality tends to be more intense than normal perceptions, revolutionary writers must plumb deeper into the unconscious than the conventional writer. Thus, the writer's task is to exhibit his own subconscious, for he is more aware—and truthful perhaps—in describing what happens:

> But in fact we already know there is no escape from ourselves. Existence is a dense plenum into which we are plunged, and every thought, wish and fear is "overdetermined," coming to be under the infinite pressures within that plenum of all other thoughts, wishes, and fears. Fingerprints and footprints are our own, and Darwin has pointed out that our inner organs differ from person to person as much as our faces. The signature of ourselves is written over all our dreams like the criminal's fingerprints across his crime. The writer, no more than any other man, can hope to escape this inescapable density of particularity. But his difference is precisely that he does not merely submit but insists upon this as his fate. It is *his own* (sic) voice which he wishes to resound in the arena of the world . . . . (Barrett 86).

According to Foster, the key to understanding *Los siete locos* is to see Erdosain as an anguished soul who could be Everyman (28). A by-product of an exploitative urban society, he is identified early in the novel when he is fired from his job for petty embezzlement and will be prosecuted unless he repays the money immediately. In an interior monologue, he reveals that he stole the money only to experience some of the city's pleasures—eat a good meal, smoke a good cigar, drink fine liqueur, and take in a movie. From the beginning, Erdosain feels excluded and unable to participate in a capitalist society. After obtaining the money to repay his employer, Erdosain, who is now unemployed, returns home only to discover that his wife Elsa is leaving him. Erdosain's misery worsens as her lover sits in the room while she packs and the three conduct an interminable conversation. When the two finally leave, Erdosain falls onto his bed and begins to fantasize about a woman he knew in his youth who he still loves. Narrating sexual fantasies was taboo in the novel of the time, and it earned harsh criticism for Arlt.

Erdosain is the kingpin around which an assortment of bizarre characters act out their lives (Leland 99). He is the epitomy of both emotional and material failure; in fact, failure becomes the motivating obsession of his existence:

> Su centro de dolor se debatía inútilmente. No encontraba en su alma una sola hendidura por donde escapar. Erdosain encerraba todo el sufrimiento del mundo, el dolor de la negación del mundo. ¿En qué parte de la tierra podía encontrarse un hombre que tuviera la piel erizada de más pliegues de amargura? Sintió que no era ya un hombre, sino una llaga cubierta de piel, que se pasmaba y gritaba a cada latido de sus venas. Y sin embargo, vivía. Vivía simultáneamente en el alejamiento y en la espantosa proximidad de su cuerpo. El ya no era un organismo envasando sufrimientos, sino algo mas inhumano—quizá eso—un monstruo enroscado en sí mismo en el negro vientre de la pieza . . . Hasta la conciencia de ser, en él no ocupaba más de un centímetro cuadrado de sensibilidad . . . El resto se desvanecía en la oscuridad . . . Lo demás había muerto en él, se había confundido con la placenta de tinieblas que blindaba su realidad atroz . . . (Arlt 57-58).

> [His center of pain throbbed uselessly, and he was unable to find in his soul a single crack through which to escape. Erdosain bore all of the world's suffering, the pain of the world's negation. Where in all the world could there be found a man whose skin bristled with more folds of bitterness? He felt that he was no longer a man but a wound covered over by skin, stunned and calling out with each throb of his veins. And yet he lived. He lived. He lived as one with the alienation and the frightening proximity of his body. He was no longer an organism brimming with sufferings but something more inhuman—perhaps that—a monster coiling in the dark womb of the room . . .Even consciousness itself occupied in him no more than a square centimeter of feeling. The rest evaporated in the darkness . . . Everything else had died in him, had become confused with the placenta of shadows that enveloped his atrocious reality.]

When his wife's wealthy cousin Barsut stops by that evening and Erdosain tells him what has happened, Barsut knocks Erdosain unconscious. Afterward, Barsut states that he is the one who denounced Erdosain for embezzlement. He had hoped Erdosain would go to jail since he had no way of repaying the money. Barsut's objective was to humiliate Elsa, who he felt had acted too proudly. He wanted to see her on her knees, begging him to help Erdosain. For the mere pleasure of hearing her be forced to say thank you, he would have given up his entire fortune. Then he could have asked her why she had stayed with Erdosain, who, to Barsut, was a fool, a coward, and a jerk. While Erdosain listens to this man tell him he is a loser, the "idea" of killing Barsut suddenly occurs to him (67).

Up to that point Erdosain is telling his story to a third party. This "Commentator," as the novel calls him, acts as a reporter, documenting the facts as Erdosain relates them and, later, providing information to the reader which Erdosain does not know. The Commentator is responsible for several footnotes along the way, the first referring to a crime:

1. Nota del Comentador: Este capítulo de las confesiones de Erdosain me hizo pensar más tarde si la idea del crímen a cometer no existiría en él en una forma subconsciente, lo que explicaría su pasividad frente a la agresión de Barsut (68).
[1. Commentator's Note: This chapter on Erdosain's confessions made me think later whether the idea of the crime he would commit did not originate in him in a subconscious manner, which would explain his passivity in reaction to Barsut's aggression.]

As Erdosain listens and his subconscious goes to work, Barsut continues his tirade, questioning why Elsa would marry such an unhappy wretch. Erdosain (who has said nothing since recovering from being hit) suddenly looks up and says: "¿Y en la cara se me nota que soy un infeliz?" (And is my facial expression that of a wretch?; 69). Barsut observes him intently and responds: "No, mirándote bien parecés un tipo agarrado por una idea fija, vaya a saber qué" (No, looking at you closely you seem obsessed by a particular idea, although I can't imagine what; 69). This is an interesting allusion to the critics who would call Arlt a fool for producing an abstract and crazy novel, but Arlt is also intent on a "particular idea."

After Barsut leaves, the frustrated Erdosain decides to visit his friend who is called the Astrologer. Waiting at a small train depot illuminated by a single light from the telegraph office, he thinks about his wife and how he will no longer pity her at home, for by then she has made love and fallen asleep on her lover's shoulder. He decides to become someone by committing a crime (71). He thinks about all the "crazy" people around him and determines he is not one of them because he is able to think and reason. There are no lights on at the Astrologer's house, but the Astrologer opens the door with a revolver in his belt and invites Erdosain into his office. Erdosain looks at a map with black flags indicating Ku Klux Klan activities in the United States. He is aware of the Astrologer's plan to develop a similar organization, and proposes a way to raise the money to put the plan into action. The Astrologer listens and becomes interested in the idea of kidnapping Barsut and holding him for ransom. They meet over subsequent days to develop Erdosain's idea. The portrayal of a mysterious and outrageous plan early in the novel leads the reader to believe this is a detective or mystery novel, which, although popular in the era, is parodied in the novel.

On an earlier visit for a loan to repay his embezzlement, Erdosain learned that the Astrologer's group needed money to start a chain of brothels which, in turn, would raise more money for the total destruction of society. Erdosain suggests using the ransom as start-up money. He becomes the protagonist of the Astrologer's plan, embarking on a nearly mystical quest as a meaningful substitute for the obsessive void in which he finds himself. He desires to transcend a destructive society which casts aside the anesthetized masses.

> ¡Sabe usted que algún día seremos como dioses? --Es lo que la gente bestia no comprende. Los han asesinado a los dioses. Pero día vendrá que bajo el sol correrán por los caminos gritando: "Lo queremos a Dios, lo necesitamos a Dios". ¡Qué bárbaros! Yo no me explico cómo lo han podido asesinar a Dios. Pero nosotros lo resucitaremos, inventaremos unos dioses hermosos, supercivilizados . . . . (234).
> [Did you know that one day we will be like gods? {Erdosain says, and the Astrologer replies:} --That is what the bestial people do not understand. They have murdered the gods. But the day will come when under the sun people will run to all paths screaming: "We want God, we need God." Such barbarians! I just cannot understand how they could have murdered God. But we will resurrect him, we will invent some beautiful and supercivilized gods . . . .]

Erdosain believes many people are unaware of the dynamics of modern society, and submit to exploitation and a dreary existence. He escapes from this fate once he becomes self-conscious; now the only answer for him is to establish a new order that will meet the needs of the obsessively aware. The Astrologer's Secret Society pretends to offer Erdosain this hope, and his ensuing fantasies and attempts to live them are a flight from the unbearable reality of his mundane existence.

During the days of plotting and kidnapping, Erdosain spends time observing those around him—other members of the Secret Society, street people, passengers in the city train station, and the women in a brothel. He also converses with his wife in his mind as he walks around the city.[ii] Meanwhile, Erdosain's life is more interesting, and he is more in touch with his surroundings than when he worked as a bookkeeper. He seems to have acquired an acute sense of living; but there is also a constant suggestion of death, and confusion as to whether certain people are dead or alive throughout the novel. On one occasion, he talks for several hours with Hipólita, his favorite prostitute, and later asks the Astrologer whether redheads can be trusted. The night before Barsut is to be killed, Erdosain lies on the bed with Hipólita while she sleeps. He strokes a revolver in his pocket and imagines how easy it would be to kill her:

> Bastaría un tiro en el cráneo. La bala es de acero y sólo haría un agujerito. Eso y se le saltarían los ojos de las órbitas y quizá la nariz echara sangre (224-225).
> [It would only take one shot in the skull. It is a steel bullet and would only make a small hole. That and her eyes would pop out of her head and perhaps her nose would bleed.]

He leans over her and cocks the pistol, but thunder suddenly crashes in the distance, then "esa extraña incoherencia que envolvía como un velo su cerebro se apartó de él" (the strange incoherence which has covered his brain like a veil lifted; 225), and he quietly gathers his things and leaves. He feels hungry and goes to a cafe, but the obsession with death does not leave him. He orders tea and rests his head against the wall as he thinks about the redhead. The waiter raises his voice saying he cannot sleep there. Erdosain is about to respond, but the waiter goes over to shake someone else who has fallen asleep, with his head resting on his crossed arms on the table. The waiter screams at him, but the man does not stir; then they discover he is dead from suicide. The police arrive. A piece of paper under his arms reveals his story, and Erdosain remembers having read it in the newspaper the day before: The man was an embezzler who left his wife and five children to live with a woman with whom he had three additional children. Then he found a seventeen-year old lover and they checked into a hotel. But that night he covered her head with a pillow and shot her because she did not want to go away with him. He stayed with her for some time and then went to the cafe, where he is found dead.

When Erdosain meets with the Astrologer later that day, he asks if he has heard about the man's story. The Astrologer says no, and several hours later totally refutes the story:

> A propósito, ¿de dónde sacó usted esa historia del suicida del café? He visto los diarios de ayer a la noche y de esta mañana. Ninguno trae esa noticia. Usted la ha soñado.
> --Sin embargo, yo puedo enseñarle el café.
> --Pues soñó en el café, entonces.
> --Puede ser, no tiene importancia . . . (238).
> [By the way, where did you get that story about the suicide in the cafe? I have looked at yesterday's afternoon papers, and this morning's edition, and none have any news about this incident. You must have dreamed it.
> --Nevertheless, I could show you the cafe.
> --Well then you dreamed in the cafe.
> --Could be, it's not important.]

This account near the end of the novel evokes Erdosain's entire situation, and perhaps his own suicidal thoughts; otherwise, it is never explained why Erdosain noted that he had read about the suicide in the newspaper while the Astrologer could not find it anywhere. None of the numerous encounters Erdosain has with other characters seem to have a purpose other than to solidify the anarchic, chaotic, and inevitable destruction of society. Arlt seems to have a "perverse curiosity" about human nature in its worst conditions (Larra 38); he prefers to press buttons and watch reactions in his characters rather than explore their personalities. Arlt's account is also interspersed with reports of actual contemporary events—war in China, strikes, political shifts—realities more depressing than his fiction.

As with the other novels in this study, the plot is less important than the characters. In *Los siete locos*, the Astrologer and leader of the Secret Society, other members called Melancholy Pimp and Gold-Seeker (Foster's translation) and, of course, Erdosain and Barsut, each deliver long monologues about their lives. In their fanatical plan to destroy modern society, the madmen decide to employ murder, prostitution, and robbery, but not without philosophizing about it. The madmen's plan, however, never comes to fruition; in fact, the reader discovers from the Commentator (although not until about two-thirds into the novel) that the Secret Society is a brilliant hoax perpetrated by the Astrologer. Erdosain never does find out; he is deadly serious in carrying out a plan of destruction that is supposed to be the ultimate solution to man's dilemma. Arlt's text is not only a parody of the novel, be it detective, psychological, or realist, but also of society and the politics manipulating international world order. In the words of the Astrologer (which are also reminiscent of late-twentieth century society):

> ¿Qué es lo que se opone aquí en la Argentina para que exista también una sociedad secreta que alcance tanto poderío como aquélla allá? Y le hablo a usted con franqueza. No sé si nuestra sociedad será bolchevique o fascista. A veces me inclino a creer que lo mejor que sé puede hacer es preparar una ensalada rusa que ni Dios la entienda. Creo que no se me puede pedir más sinceridad en este momento. Vea que por ahora lo que yo pretendo hacer es un bloque donde se consoliden todas las posibles esperanzas humanas. Mi plan es dirigirnos con preferencia a los jóvenes bolcheviques, estudiantes y proletarios inteligentes. Además, acogeremos a los que tienen un plan para reformar el universo, a los empleados que aspiran a ser millonarios, a los inventores fallados . . . a los cesantes de cualquier cosa, a los que acaban de sufrir un proceso y quedan en la calle sin saber para qué lado mirar (31).
>
> [What is there to prevent the existence here, in Argentina, of a secret society just as powerful as [the Ku Klux Klan]? Understand that I am speaking in all candor. I do not know if our society will be bolshevik or fascist. At times I am inclined to believe that it would be best to put together a Russian salad that not even God would understand. I do not think you can ask me to be any more sincere than I am being right now. But note that for now what I want to do is put together a unit that will consolidate all human hopes. My plan is for us to address ourselves preferably to young bolsheviks, students, intelligent proletarians. Moreover, we can count on appealing to anyone with a plan to reform the universe, to employees that want to be millionaires, to inventors who have failed . . . to anyone who has ever been fired, to people who have just been through a trial and are out in the cold not knowing where to turn.]

Erdosain learns, in the meetings of the Secret Society, the supposed true nature of a new order. However, the society sardonically offered by *Los siete locos* is aligned with the totalitarian social gospels prevalent in the late 1920s (Foster 33). This new society, a brotherhood, provides its members with identity and a sense of organization. The greatest irony, however, is that Erdosain does not seem to realize that the objectives of the society are precisely those of the world which he feels has repulsively cast him aside and from which he is fleeing. If the alternative to western capitalism is only a similar order, a need still exists for self-identity.

Los siete locos condemns modern totalitarian structures, and some of the characters help represent the technological necessities of a modern city—streetcars, trains, telephones, bureaucracy. Others represent the abstract philosophies of a changing world. Hopelessness and pessimism follow industrialism, communism, futurism, and fascism, making it impossible to have faith in anything. There is an obsessive search for a god that is insupportably absent, but the frustration is also with a reality that distorts and lies. Humankind, like Arlt's protagonist, must escape into fantasy in order to survive; the novelist uses fantasy along with new structures and styles to reveal the malaise of the era he is trying to recreate:

> It is not at the level of concepts that the appalling face of the world is seen; it is another kind of meaning that the writer must construct . . . . He must put forth those works which look back into his gaze with conviction and authenticity and wear about them the gleams of interest (Barrett 98).

In his novel, Arlt resorts to shifting points of view, chaotic monologues, and alternating time and space, or Bakhtinian chronotopes, such as meeting/parting (separation), loss/acquisition, search/discovery, recognition/nonrecognition (Bakhtin 97). Although supposedly chronological, it is not clear whether some events are imagined. It is often confusing as to who narrates—an omniscient narrator, a commentary on Erdosain's oral and written confessions, Erdosain's own voice, or Elsa's thoughts. In addition, every few pages the narration stops for a footnote or makes reference to what is contained in an unwritten future novel. This technique can cause confusion, and some critics during Arlt's time, who expected a linear structure, were baffled by the contradictions within the text. For some, Arlt did not know how to structure his writing, and he was grammatically incorrect:

> [Ese descarriado ojo novelístico parece pertenecer también a uno de los locos de la novela. La prosa es torpe y en ocasiones ilegible (Anderson Imbert 301).
> That askewed novelistic eye seems to belong to one of the lunatics in the novel. The prose is awkward and at times illegible.]

But in time, Arlt's technique would be called extremely innovative, and he would be deemed "prophetic" (Anderson Imbert 302), not only for his technique but also for his subject matter (hate, violence, sex, crime, illness, and cynicism). In his postmodern novel, *Respiración Artificial* (Artificial Respiration; 1980), Argentinian novelist Ricardo Piglia cites and, in a way, eulogizes Arlt's attempt to revise narrative strategies. In Piglia's novel, two characters discuss how Arlt has been considered a bad writer, but then one adds:

Cualquier maestra de la escuela primaria, incluso mi tía Margarita, dijo
Renzi, puede corregir una página de Arlt, pero nadie puede escribirla,
salvo él (137).
[Any grade school teacher, including my Aunt Margaret, Renzi said,
could correct one of Arlt's pages, but no one could write it, except him.]

They continue discussing his style, and determine his legacy in
literature:

Arlt escribe contra la idea de estilo literario, o sea, contra lo que nos
enseñaron que debía entenderse por escribir bien, esto es, escribir
pulcro, prolijito, sin gerundios, sin palabras repetidas. Por eso el mejor
elogio que puede hacerse de Arlt es decir que en sus mejores momentos
es ilegible; al menos los críticos dicen que es ilegible: no lo pueden
leer, desde su código no lo pueden leer. El estilo de Arlt, dijo Renzi, es
lo reprimido de la literatura argentina. Todos los críticos . . . están de
acuerdo en una sola cosa: en decir que escribía mal. . . . Tienen razón,
dado que Arlt no escribía desde el mismo lugar que ellos, ni tampoco
desde el mismo código. Y en esto Arlt es absolutamente moderno:
está más adelante que todos esos chitrulos que lo acusan (137-138).
[Arlt writes against the idea of literary style, in other words, against
that which was taught us which should be understood as writing well,
that is, writing neat, tediously, without gerunds, without repeated
words. That is why the best praise that can be made of Arlt is to say
that in his better moments he is illegible, at least the critics say he is
illegible: they cannot read him, they cannot interpret his code. Arlt's
style, Renzi said, is the repressed of Argentine literature. All the critics
. . . are agreed on one aspect: in stating that he wrote badly. . . .They
were right, given that Arlt did not write from the same place as they,
nor from the same code. In this Arlt is completely modern: he is ahead
of all those imbeciles who accuse him.]

According to Piglia's characters, the critics who thought Arlt wrote
poorly did not understand what he was doing—completely revamping,
changing, and modernizing narrative style. Piglia's characters decide
that no writer in this century has been as innovative as Arlt; in fact,
they convincingly exclude Borges from being a part of the birth of
contemporary literature:

Con la muerte de Arlt en 1942 . . . se terminó la literatura moderna en
la Argentina, lo que sigue es un páramo sombrío. Con él, ¿terminó
todo? dijo Marconi. ¿Qué tal? ¿Y Borges? Borges, dijo Renzi, es un
escritor del siglo XIX. El mejor escritor argentino del siglo XIX (133).
[With Arlt's death in 1942 . . . modern literature in Argentina ended,
what follows is a gloomy drizzle. With him, everything ended?

Marconi said. Really? What about Borges?Borges, Renzi said, is a
writer from the nineteenth century. The best Argentine writer of the
nineteenth century.]

One purpose of Piglia's novel is to critique contemporary literature.
Its relationship to history, traditional criticism, and the eternal search
for an Argentine identity, are all reflected in his novel's dualistic
structure as a schizophrenic conflict between European civilization and
the *criollo* (Creole) tradition of a barbaric hinterland (Menton 126).
Piglia's novel is even considered the novel Borges never wrote, a
narration in which action is minimal and intellectual monologues,
dialogues, and letters predominate. Piglia's theme is the impossiblity of
arriving at the absolute truth, of either history or contemporary reality,
because everything is "artificial" (Menton 129). Piglia, coming to a
conclusion similar to his predecessor's, credits Arlt for seeing the need
to recreate and redefine the novel genre, and embarks on his own
discourse much in the style of Arlt.

If Arlt's writing was not "bad" but innovative, what was his
purpose? In discussing the language of the avant-garde, English critic
Raymond Williams notes the artist's need to linguistically portray the
"inner form" of a word, its internal creative capacity (38). The
Vanguardia artist sought to go beyond the futuristic rejection of the past
and the Dadaistic freeing of words, to a revelatory expression. The
Russian Formalists' concept of the word as a grammatical unit or (in
Expressionistic terms) a transrational sound element showed the
literary element or potential. This is the dichotomy of the Vanguardia
novel:

> Whether as 'grammatical unit' or as 'transrational sound image' [the
> word] can be projected in two quite different directions: on the one
> hand towards active composition, in which these units are arranged and
> combined, by conscious literary strategies or devices, into works; or, on
> the other hand, taking an ideological cue from 'transrational', into
> procedures much resembling traditional accounts of 'inspiration', in
> which the creative act occurs beyond the 'ordinary self' and more
> substantial, more original, energies are tapped (39).

While a muse may be a conventional way to describe creative
access to the subconscious (a human state newly defined by Freud), the
innovative writer tries to show artistic inspiration to creation without
resorting to older, outmoded strategies, i.e., the artist's possession by
gods or spirits, inspiring muses or ancestor poets, the personification of
Nature, or even the automatic writing of their peers. Since language
consistently blocks true consciousness, the writer sought to unblock

and reveal pure consciousness. This could only occur if a new idea were represented. Whereas Arqueles Vela transformed the Modernista muse to a technological muse in *El café de nadie*, Roberto Arlt uses madness in plot and structure to show his artistic inspiration. His goal was to open consciousness, but he was completely misunderstood because he was showing rather than telling. The madmen of this novel lead the way through an insane tale (which is a ruse) designed to stir up the experiences which prompt artistic creation. The plot is not the tale itself but the whirlwind in which the reader finds himself, a strange, unidentified mental space from which inspiration must come.

Fragmentation aids the chaotic feeling of *Los siete locos*. The book is about 230 pages in length, and is divided into three sections without titles. However, several chapters within each section carry titles that denote the action or lack of action therein, for example: The surprise; States of consciousness; To be by means of a crime; Incoherences; The black house; The interior life; Sensation of the subconscious; and, The revelation (all titles my translation). As with his footnotes, which serve to confuse rather than clarify, Arlt does not tantalize the reader with subtitles, instead he gives away the general plot. The fragmented structure drives Arlt's episodic discourse, which emulates soap opera style. Popular in his day, the radio soap opera built plot in suspense or mystery. Arlt's story of a poor man who has embezzled from his employer, is threatened with prosecution, and whose wife finds a lover and leaves him, is dramatic soap opera. The suspense builds as Erdosain tries to find money, and plots to kill a wealthy enemy who also fancied his wife. The Astrologer and his strange friends, the prostitutes and street people, all add to the drama. But this soap opera has no conclusion; the end is chaotic and frustrating, and the reader is never told what happened. The reader can either decide the novel has a incompetent writer; or, he/she can think about the artist's intention, see the parody of soap opera format, the critique of the conventional novel, and Arlt's political commentary.

Arlt's vision of modern urban life as the enemy of society was similar to that of his peers T.S. Eliot and James Joyce. Although a return to the past is impossible, Arlt construes it as a viable option in *Los siete locos*. His desire is for a return to genuine Argentine roots, as well as to the genuine creative consciousness for the artist. The novel must return to its origins, just as people and politics had attempted to accomplish with the Russian Revolution. If artists reject old form (as society had with old monarchies and rules), they can breathe new life into narrative fiction, as the Boedo group announced in manifestos. From there, inspiration and creation—however mad they seem upon inception—will follow. Arlt grew up in lower class society and distrusted elitist literature modeled on earlier convention. He knew the conventional model would not reveal the deepest human and artistic consciousness, so unrecognized that it became a state of madness (Lindstrom 79). Arlt called attention to his discourse by the distortion and chronotopic characteristics of his narrative fiction. Thus, his novel is more metaphysical than political.

Transgressing limits can produce ruptured and fragmented images that elude classification, just as some contemporary narratives by women deliberately break with traditional sequences. According to Roland Barthes, such a process evades closure imposed by traditional plot; it provides a way to break out and become innovative. Arlt's fragmentation becomes a creative tool and triggers the fertile multiplicity of identities. Through writing comes reinvention, and Arlt, along with other Vanguardia writers, was one of the first in this century to reinvent the novel. The act of reshaping narrative structure is foremost in much contemporary narrative; in fact, recent criticism says novels such as Julio Cortázar's *Rayuela* (1963; *Hopscotch*, 1968) would not have been possible without precursors such as *Los siete locos*:

> The Romantic novel . . . various generations of Romantic novelists . . .
> is an articulate and coherent body of work. That is precisely what we
> encounter with these new Latin American novelists, who already stem
> from each other: Cortázar from Marechal, from Borges, from Arlt . . .
> (Fernández Retamar 250).

This critic acknowledges the contributions to the contemporary novel of succeeding generations of Argentine writers, beginning with Roberto Arlt. In the following, a critic more specifically seeks a thread uniting Argentine writers by the "mark" left on them from previous generations:

> What I am interested in stressing now is what unites [new twentieth
> century novelists]. In the first place, I would say, it is the mark left on
> their work by the masters of the previous group of writers. To give a
> single example: what would *Hopscotch*, that quintessentially Argentine
> novel which *Hopscotch* is beneath its French patina, be without
> Macedonio Fernández, without Borges, without Roberto Arlt, without
> Marechal, without Onetti? . . .(Rodríguez Monegal 106).

As in Arlt's plays, strong existentialist aspects in *Los siete locos* underscore his style and discourse. Although some critics have seen traits of Naturalism—a popular form in Latin America in the early years of the century, which minutely described the ugly side of life—in this novel, it is instead an example of Existentialism. What would seem to be naturalistic elements serve only to propagate his Existential discourse (Foster 23). The ugliness of Erdosain's society critiques an era of total chaos. In Erdosain, Arlt achieves the certainty of being both judge and a part of his own absurdity. Erdosain, as well as the artist, is a victim of both interior and exterior. While the hoax perpetrated on Erdosain provides him with a sense of identity and importance, his inability to comprehend that he is perpetuating the society he rejected undermines any permanent value for the hoax. Similarly, repeating the actions of the conventional novel serves no constructive purpose. Arlt, the artist, both learns from and destroys his character (a semblance of the traditional character).

All of Arlt's characters seek the solitude of a simpler life they can control. By annihilating everything, they hope to find peace. Incongruous as that may seem, their chaotic actions reflect the rapid and repeated changes in states of consciousness that occur in artistic impetus. Artistic moods can be cynical, self-compassionate, and sado-masochistic much like these characters' dispositions. Various states of consciousness are inherent in the development of life, and the search for identity, as well as the creative process. A common topic in Argentina in this period was that of the nation in a state of orphanhood, seeking its true identity. Erdosain thinks he is an orphan, thus accentuating his solitary and alienated existence. Arlt alienates his text, seeks an escape from stagnant novelistic form, and discovers the true consciousness of the artist. He creates the new Argentine novel.

In *Los siete locos*, Erdosain is elevated to the level of a martyr figure who thinks he will save his soul and all mankind through his commitment to the new order, even though it involves murder. This gives meaning to Erdosain's otherwise empty existence. For Arlt and possibly for the reader, society is simply a cruel fascist hoax to exploit the helpless, all of which points to the ultimate irony, that is, the tension between the knowledge of the reader and the lack of that same knowledge by Erdosain. Resolution, for the reader, comes in knowing the futility of transcendent orders, the paradox of the human quest for them, and the inescapable truth that if they do not exist (as with God), society will create them (Foster 37)—a concept developed by Bertold Brecht in his plays of the late 1920s. Irony, a key point of *Los siete locos*, is a powerful, apolitical tool wielded against authority (Hutcheon 1994, 27). Arlt, like the other novelists of this study, achieves the duality of socio-political commentary and showing the way toward new narrative strategies.

Throughout, several items are never clarified: Who exactly are the seven madmen? Does the Astrologer finally explain to Erdosain that he did not have Barsut killed after all? Will Erdosain go to jail as he believes when he hides with the commentator and tells his story? If these things do not matter, is the purpose of the story to get the reader to think, to see himself as Erdosain, neither a madman nor a savior, but a complex human consciousness?

The novel, in fact, ends with these two lines:

> --Sabe que usted se parece a Lenin?
> Y antes de que el Astrólogo pudiera contestarle, salió (Arlt 239).
> [--Did you know that you look like Lenin?
> But before the Astrologer could answer, [Erdosain] left.]

It is of note that Arlt makes a comparison in 1929 to a revolutionary figure, Vladimir Lenin, several years dead (the Russian philosopher and leader of the Bolsheviks was virtually incapacitated by a stroke in 1922 and died in January 1924). By then, Russian Bolshevism was also dead and Joseph Stalin had risen to power, bringing a new philosophy to the Soviet Union. Whether they were fascists, communists, or capitalists, reigning philosophies fell by the wayside, but not without first impacting their societies in the 1920s. In *Los siete locos*, the Astrologer is the philosopher and reigning power—he controls the hoax pulled on Erdosain, he holds Barsut's life in his hands, and he knows whether something has happened or if Erdosain simply dreamed it. In spite of the Commentator, the Astrologer also seems to control the story—until the end. Then Erdosain, the foolish character, informs the Astrologer that he looks like the dead leader of a failed revolution and walks away without allowing him to respond or control the story. Now the Astrologer is left looking like a fool; he cannot make his usual wisecracks or dominate the situation. If the Astrologer is representative of the artist, as Foster believes, Arlt demonstrates here that the artist has now lost control of his own creation. The character he controlled and made a fool of just walked away with final control of his destiny and the novel's destiny. Arlt proposes to portray more than the hopeless, demoralized state of society; he wants to show that new perspectives can emerge from chaos. The artist needs to lose control. Foolishness and lack of control (or lack of paradigms) in prose fiction is good for it leads to a more pure creation.

The world in *Los siete locos* is a labyrinth without an exit. Anguish arises from the concept of existence in the universe, but it can also arise from the artistic act of devouring and replacing the previous artistic/creative generation. Parody and irony are essential to the dialogic process, but expressing dislocation or distortion is only part of it. The realization of the overwhelming role of irony in the novel and the particular form that this irony assumes is ultimately what the critics did not grasp and why, decades later, Ricardo Piglia thought it necessary to make this point for postmodern literature. The structural contradictions, especially the supposed omniscient narrator's participation in the action, invited doubts as to Arlt's competence as a writer (Foster 44). If Arlt's novel were only a statement on the unacceptable circumstances of the lower classes, and their need for a belief in transcendent promises, *Los siete locos* would be a social realist novel. But it is much more innovative. Erdosain is not simply a disenchanted Everyman seeking escape from the urban, political world, he is the creative product at the hands of a perhaps maniacal artist seeking ultimate expression. There is no better "artist" than the Astrologer to make this statement (Foster 44). The artist (Astrologer) offers the character (Erdosain) a "new order," the hope of new meaning (in the genre). In Arlt's new order, the character finds a greater sense of life, by seeking to establish meaning in his existence. The artist controls that expression, until he loses it to the character, that is to say, to artistic expression itself.

Because of its strangeness, the Vanguardia novel has remained marginalized from the traditional literary canon of its day, that is, the popular realist, indigenista or lyrical novel. Its structure is confusing with its stylistic errors, a seeming lack of completion, and the resulting chaos in plot. Innovation can be misunderstood when it is so puzzling. *Los siete locos* is innovative for its structure, dialogue, plot, the use of characters and, especially, in its discourse. Recent studies show that the Vanguardia novel seeks to speak for narrative itself, occupy its very space, re-colonize known territory, and assume its own power (Pérez Firmat 33). Arlt's fiction accomplished these goals, although critics of his day did not identify his novel's newness.

In contrast to Eduardo Mallea, who continued to believe in the necessity of somehow creating significant meanings, Arlt is the forerunner of writers Julio Cortázar and Ernesto Sábato for his convoluted structure, abstractions, and metafiction (Foster 43). The complexity of human consciousness drives the plot in all of Arlt's narrative, and this novel is a good example of the artist in direct creative action.

In Arlt's first novel, *El juguete rabioso* (The Rabid Toy; 1927), analyzed by Vicky Unruh in her recent study on Vanguardia novelists, *The Latin American Vanguards* (1994), he synthesizes concerns that shaped activities of the two principal artistic groups, Florida and Boedo. Class and cultural conflict in this earlier novel evoke the 1920s and a call for socially-committed art. Although the narrator identifies the text as his written memoirs, the temporal relationship between the story and its telling remains vague. While narrated by an older Silvio-writer, the plot mainly consists of key moments in Silvio's life between his fourteenth and seventeenth birthdays. The youth dreams of fame and thereby a coherent sense of self and transcendence over the persistent need to make a living in a sordid urban world; but his reality only includes scandalous and illegal activities with his friends (intellectual group with a radical agenda) and mounting frustration as he is dismissed from various career training ventures. He wanders around the city and attempts suicide. Finally, he begins to master city life, plots a robbery, and finds work through the would-be victim because of his impressive zest for life. Relocated in a new job in southern Argentina, Silvio writes his memoirs.

While *El juguete rabioso* could also be cited as a forerunner to the new narrative, Unruh is more concerned with the novel as a "construction of a specifically vanguardist artist" who has a contentious relationship with not only an artistic tradition but also a concrete world in Buenos Aires (85). Silvio's propensity to model his life on his readings situates the novel in a Bakhtinian "auto-criticism of discourse" or a testing of literary discourse by means of a character who sees the world through literature and attempts to live accordingly. *El juguete rabioso*'s discourse is not only Silvio's emerging artistic persona, but also the novel's response to the conflictive relationship between artistic inspiration and creation.

Thus, Arlt had a similar objective in both his first and second novels, which was to identify the method to his madness, or the Vanguardia artist's effort to renew the novel. (Non)identity, (un)reality, and (in)sanity are at par with each other in Arlt's world because they are at the root of human consciousness. Making this revelation to society was an effort of innovative Western writers in the 1920s, but many Latin American writers were still following conventional narrative form. Roberto Arlt, a member of Vanguardia, launched this artistic search for Argentine writers, and his novels are precursors to the great works of Argentinian twentieth century. But it is only in recent years that his contribution to later literature is being recognized.

---

[i] In an interview with Elena Poniatowska in 1976 (collected in her 1990 text *Todo México, Tomo I*; page 117), Borges quips, "¡Mallea? Ese pasó de la nada a la nada." [Mallea? He went from nothing to nothing.]

[ii] In the sequel novel, *Los lanzallamas* (1931; The Flamethrowers), Elsa goes to a convent to get over her guilt and Erdosain commits suicide.

CHAPTER FOUR

THE REBELLION OF THE ECUADOREAN CHARACTER

For Ecuador, the twentieth century began with renovation in culture and literature as well as in politics and economics. Then, in the political turbulence of the second and third decades, literature became strangled (Fernández 23). A rich, albeit small, *Vanguardia* movement arose from this period which has received only slight critical attention. Vanguardia artists influenced the writers of Social Realism of the 1930s, but their own literary contributions have yet to be recognized except by two or three critics.

Although smaller in number than many of their Latin American contemporaries, the Ecuadorean Vanguardia artists aspired to similar goals as the other writers, that is, to create new fiction that represented the Americas (Forster 8). But the Ecuadoreans had a few more handicaps than their neighbors in more populous cities. The Andean republics, after the turn of the century, struggled between two cultures, one stemming from the Spanish tradition, and the other from an indigenous past. It was more difficult to merge the two than in Mexico, where those united in revolution sought greater equality for mixed-race people, and in Argentina, where an awareness of the values of a rural community connected with the *gaucho* seemed to strengthen the populace. Still, this struggle between cultures in Ecuador took a back seat to constant border wars.

Bolivia, Peru and Ecuador are divided into diverse geographical regions, from high plateaus and tropical jungles to lowlands and coastal areas. In Ecuador sharp rivalries existed between mountain cultures and coastal societies, between Quito (in the northern highlands) and Guayaquil (in the south on the coast and traditionally more liberal from a commercial and political standpoint). Despite the achievements of novelists Juan Montalvo (1832-1889), Benjamín Carrión (1897-1979), Jorge Icaza (1906-1978), and Jorge Enrique Adoum (1923-), Ecuador, like Bolivia, has always provided a more challenging cultural environment for writers (compared to Mexico City or Buenos Aires), mainly due to isolation, frequent wars, and poor economic progress (Fernández 27).[i]

At independence, Ecuador's population was mostly Indian and *mestizo* (mixed Spanish/Indian race), of which the majority lived in the rural areas while those of Spanish or European ancestry lived in the cities. Fewer people, including some of African heritage, lived in the coastal lowlands. Difficult terrain and climate slowed modernization; in fact, for more than a century, Ecuador was one of the least modernized countries of Latin America (Franco 1967, 254).

Bordered on the north by Colombia and on the south by Peru—each more than twice its size—Ecuadoreans spent the early decades of the twentieth century fighting with their southern neighbor over bordering territories. By 1942, at the urging of Argentina, Brazil, Chile, and the United States, Ecuador accepted a boundary treaty favorable to Peru, to end the incessant war. Its territory was much reduced from original claims, and denunciation of the 1942 accord would become a tradition of later Ecuadorean politicians.

Presidents changing frequently in these early decades hindered progress and a stable government. While conservatives and liberals fought each other in the cities at the turn of the century and into the next two decades, the Indian population continued to live in the high mountains, on poor land, and subject to a variety of abuses by government and absent landlords. They had no voice in politics. Although political leaders continued to ignore this abominable human rights situation, realist narrative fiction committed to Indian themes surged in the 1930s, finally calling attention to the plight of non-European people. The subsequent popularity of indigenista fiction, then, completely overshadowed the achievements of the Vanguardia artists of the 1920s (Fernández 15), who first opened narrative to an evaluation of their society. The innovations of an Ecuadorean Vanguardia are barely noted in English-language criticism. References to his work seldom appear in recent critical texts, and yet a few critics are beginning to recognize Pablo Palacio (1906-1946) for his accomplishment in renovating prose fiction and the twentieth century novel in Ecuador.

Despite wars and political problems, this country slowly began to modernize. Whereas Ecuador's economy had been the worst in Latin America, by the late 1910s an economic boom began to take place in the cities, mainly because of cacao exportation that began early in the century. The economy was dependent mainly on bananas, cacao, and coffee, three food products subject to price fluctuations in the world market (Franco 1967, 254). At the turn of the twentieth century, a railway was built and put into operation between Guayaquil and Quito. Education expanded in the cities and labor was organized for a short time (a general strike paralyzed Guayaquil in November, 1922, and other strikes took place in several cities for months afterward), but the country was too weak to defend outlying territories during the early decades (Fernández 42).

These problems of race, poverty, and wars did not help build a strong literary community. However—although Ecuadorean writers of the early century are noted for their Realism, especially in the indigenista novel—an avant-garde movement took place in Guayaquil and Quito as in other Latin American cities, which renovated language and structure in both poetry and narrative fiction (Forster 184). Urban writers were influenced by the Argentinian Ultraísmo and the avant-garde movements in Europe, often elaborated by other South Americans in literary journals (although the avant-garde first entered Ecuador as "Futurism" in 1919). Increased educational opportunities and student activism often created poets or inspired other intellectuals. Hugo Mayo (née Miguel Augusto Egas; 1898-1988) was a central figure of the early Vanguardia movement, noted for his original personality and poetry (Anderson Imbert 47). He and other innovators published in several avant-garde journals: *Síngulus* (1921), *Proteo* (1922), and *Iniciación* (1921-1927). The editors of *Iniciación* sought contributions, in addition to a new esthetic, of new themes based on film, aviation, velocity, and industry or machine-like qualities (Fernández 37). Many of these poets chose esthetic over Ecuadorean themes, wanting "to renovate or to die" (36).

The "Guayaquil Group" won international recognition and consisted of younger, realistic novelists and a major poet, Jorge Carrera Andrade (1902-1978), who were greatly influenced by both Hugo Mayo writings and Pablo Palacio's prose fiction and short drama (Unruh 17). This group's prose fiction and the Social Realism of the 1930s are often considered the Ecuadorean offspring of initial innovations of Vanguardia for their discourse, structure, and language.

But the early innovators have also been overshadowed by those who followed. Two recent texts—María del Carmen Fernández' *El realismo abierto de Pablo Palacio en la encrucijada de los 30* (Pablo Palacio's Open Realism at the Crossroads of the 30s; 1991), and Humberto E. Robles' *La noción de vanguardia en el Ecuador* (The Notion of Vanguard in Ecuador; 1989)—have been helpful in pointing out the nearly forgotten impact of the Vanguardia in Ecuador which, although less extensive and enduring than movements in Argentina, Peru, Chile, Cuba, and Brazil, affected subsequent artistic generations. No in-depth study on Palacio exists in English. In her study on the movement, Vicky Unruh characterizes Ecuador's vanguardista activity as "a sustained debate about the pertinence of the new, international artistic currents to the country's cultural situation" (18). She agrees with Robles' argument that polarized positions between classical and socially-committed concepts of art allowed for little middle ground, resulting in an emphasis on socially-oriented art in the 1930s.

The artists of the 1920s tended to support revolutionary political parties, but even these changed from year to year. In 1919, an economic crisis occurred when cacao prices abroad dropped substantially; for the next two years, as the budding economy wilted, demonstrations and strikes escalated nationwide. By 1923, farmworkers were striking in outlying areas, leading to peasant massacre. The middle-class tightened its belt, but the lower classes felt the impact the most. An insurrection by the military occurred in July 1925, called the *Tenientes* (lieutenants') or July revolution, which influenced avant-garde writing (Fernández 43). After the revolt, young writers and poets discovered that their writings no longer expressed the realities of their generation. At the same time, the Ecuadorean Vanguardia had split into two groups: a formal group that sought to discover new esthetic values in poetry, following Dadaist and Ultraist concepts, and a group that wanted to reveal true Ecuadorean reality through an examination of social and economic conditions. After 1925, a new political-cultural ambience began to spread which sought to develop the July revolution's initial ideas—to modernize state institutions and overthrow the power of the previous generation's plutocratic patriarchy. Socialist military forces and the judicial court sought to instill equality for all, provide dignity for the indigenous race, and enact efficient laws to help workers (Fernández 45). But this administration was not able to put its ideas into practice.

The middle class gained banking and economic control, and many Ecuadorean intellectuals soon became disenchanted with the ideals of the Lieutenants' revolution. They accused the instigators of tyranny. Now a more conservative group, including the clerical orders, took control of the government. The Socialist party was blamed for stonewalling much-needed reforms, and the Indians and poor did not see a change in their situations. A dictatorship followed, but, by the mid-1930s, politics stabilized again and many writers and poets had taken up the plight of the indigenous and black populations (Franco 1967, 113). First, however, the roots of the Social Realism novel (not to be confused with the realist novel that was popular in the late nineteenth and early twentieth centuries) formed in a few early novels and Vanguardia narrative.

At the turn of the twentieth century, Ecuador, like many other Hispanic American countries, responded to Uruguayan José Enrique Rodó's (1871-1917) cry for revelation of the true race and art of the Americas (*Ariel*, 1900). Rodó associated capitalism with foreign (especially United States) control over Latin American countries; city life and a dependence on an international economy were considered anti-Hispanic.

Ecuador's first novel to encompass an understanding of the problems, including foreign involvement, was Luis Martínez's *A la costa* (To the Coast; 1904). The protagonist is a poor law student whose studies are interrupted by civil war, during which he earns a living as a shop assistant and works at various menial jobs. His friend, the son of a landowner, also abandons his studies but leaves Quito to work on his father's coastal plantation. The healthy life on the land is contrasted with the protagonist's frustrations in the capital—dependent on foreign exports—which finally drive him also, to the land, where he wins respect as the good-hearted foreman of a banana plantation. This novel effectively portrays the message that one must break out of the constricting life in the city if one is to understand the country as a whole. *A la costa* had little impact until 1930, when social realist writers gave credit to Martínez's literary theme and style (Franco 1967, 256).

Benjamín Carrión's account of the failed life of an intellectual, *El desencanto de Miguel García* (Miguel García's Disenchantment; 1926) touched on a Vanguardia theme: the plight of the intellectual and artist aspiring to renovate the novel. The Ecaudorean indigenista novel—which Jorge Icaza (1906-1978) would memorialize with *Huasipungo* in 1934—was born in Fernando Cháves' (1902-1991) account of the suffering of Indians under the injustice of priests and feudal landowners, called *Plata y bronce* (Silver and Bronze; 1927). However, neither García's nor Cháves' texts truly changed the structure or plot of the modern novel.

During the 1920s, artists became aware of the latest in the French avant-garde, Surrealism, by means of two journals from Spain, *Revista de Occidente* (1923-36) and *La Gaceta Literaria* (1927-32). But Surrealism by the late 1920s fell out with the political ideology it had espoused, Communism, and Latin American artists sought ways to merge new ideologies and the desire to regenerate artistic creativity. Local journals called for an autonomous innovative creation in true Ecuadorean spirit (Robles 41):

> La literatura vanguardista va cediendo el paso a la verdadera literatura
> de vanguardia, que recoge sus vibraciones inéditas del caudal de la
> Vida—real, humana, palpitante (44).
> [Vanguardista literature begins opening the way to the true literature of
> vanguardia, which gathers its unpublished vibrations from the
> abundance of Life--real, human, palpitating.]

The European avant-garde served only as inspiration; Ecuadorean artists in the 1920s had no intention of imitating Europe. They were tired of the previous century's French Romanticism, which was still popular in Latin American literature. The Vanguardia artists believed in Rodó's call for a representation of the *Americano,* or spirit of the American continent. With politics and capitalism following Eurocentric models, some artists sought to rebel from a literary tradition linked to the dominant economic and political powers. While Hugo Mayo and others began a revolution in poetry, Fernando Cháves and Pablo Palacio emerged with new narrative fiction in 1927; Cháves worked with new themes, and Palacio incorporated new structures and discourses.

Palacio had published several short works in journals since 1920, but his first book was published in his second year at the university in Quito. *Un hombre muerto a_puntapiés* (A Man Killed by Kicking; 1927). It is a collection of nine texts which elicited noticeable commentary for their strange content. Even the title was provoking and confusing; Palacio's uncle (who had raised him), upon first seeing an article about the book in the newspaper, thought his nephew was the culprit who had kicked a man to death (Flores Jaramillo 38). That same year, 21-year-old Palacio published *Débora,* and became the talk of the town. No other writer of the 1920s would be received with equal amazement and consternation. These two dehumanized, anti-sentimental novels were followed by another remarkable, novel, *Vida de un ahorcado* (Life of a Hanged Man; 1932), which completed Palacio's project of creating the antinovel. The latter was his strongest attack on middle-class society.

Enrique Anderson Imbert calls Palacio "an excellent monologuer;" the artist chose this technique long before other authors used it to reveal interior realities (262). *Débora* consists of two crisscrossing monologues: one is the character's, who wanders about the city of Quito hoping and waiting to have a romantic liaison, and the second belongs to the narrator/author, who reflects on the novel in general and the process of creating the novel. It is an anguished narrative—anguish felt by both the character and the author—with no final resolution. Indeed, the "Deborah" longed for by the main character never appears and is named only in the final fragment. Her name conjures the idea of the biblical prophetess Deborah. This character, simply called "the Lieutenant," may be waiting for her to save him from his frustration of never finding a perfect love, perfect salvation, or even the perfect artistic creation. The discourse shows hope and anguish for the modern novel, which is similar to his hope for improvement in his socio-political moment (politically, Palacio was a member of the new Socialist party in Quito). Frequent transitions from the character's freedom to develop his story and the narrator's comments on writing, further Palacio's ideas on prose fiction.

The essential plot of *Débora*, then, concerns a character that has not yet fully left the artist's head. As he tries to go about his development (or life)—talking to another character called Lieutenant B, visiting the uglier side of town, or getting up and ready in the morning—he is regularly interrupted by the narrator's commentary on him. The novel ends because the narrator has the Lieutenant die, thereby neglecting traditional character development. Or so Palacio would have the reader believe.

Although commentary on Palacio's urban society is apparent in *Débora*, and even political denunciation with his use of a character called only "the Lieutenant" (most likely after the lieutenants' revolt of 1925), his greater accomplishment is his criticism of the logic, structure, and rules of the conventional novel—similar to Arqueles Vela's intention. Palacio's generation was not ready for this change. Ecuadorean critic Angel Rojas said Palacio's literature was "difficult," and too intellectualized, and Luis Alberto Sánchez called him a great frustrated lyric (Rojas 22-23). Although the critics understood *Débora* to be a manifesto on how to write the novel, they surmised that readers would not understand its purpose (Pareja Diez Canseco 103-104).

Palacio's novel is a characterization of art and an attack on the romantic and realist novels of the previous century. It agonizes over the rules of logic of the traditional novel by having the narrator voice them as the characters are being shaped (Rivas Iturralde 22). A Vanguardia artist, Palacio saw that new politics, science, and a modern society all precipitated the novel's need to change. He supplants traditional form with a new form brought to life by the narrator, who speaks with the authority of the artist as he shapes, or abstains from shaping, the traditional character, the Lieutenant.

The narrator (or the novel in the making) ironizes:

¿A quién le va a interesar que las medias del Teniente están rotas y que esto constituye una de sus más fuertes tragedias, el desequilibrio esencial de su espíritu? ¿A quién le interesa la relación de que en la mañana, al levantarse, se quedó veinte minutos sobre la cama, cortándose tres callos y acomodándose las uñas? (Palacio 72)

[Who is going to be interested in the fact that the Lieutenant's hose are torn and that this constitutes one of his greatest tragedies, that essential disequilibrium of his spirit? Who would be interested in the account that in the morning, upon getting up, he spends twenty minutes sitting on the bed, cutting three callouses and trimming his toenails?]

Then Palacio is more direct:

La novela realista engaña lastimosamente. Abstrae los hechos y deja el campo lleno de vacíos; les da una continuidad imposible, porque lo verídico, lo que se calla, no interesaría a nadie (72).
[The realist novel deceives hurtfully. It abstracts the facts and leaves the field open to emptiness; it gives them an impossible continuity, because the veridic, what would be quieted, does not interest anyone.]

Here Palacio implies that the traditional artist sought to show reality, but when all was said and done, he did not achieve it:

Sucede que se tomaron las realidades grandes, voluminosas; y se callaron las pequeñas realidades, por inútiles. Pero las realidades pequeñas son las que, acumulándose, constituyen una vida . . . La verdad: casi nunca se da en el caso, aunque sea muy posible. Mentiras, mentiras y mentiras (72).
[It so happens that they took the big, voluminous realities, and squelched the little realities, saying they were useless. But the little realities are the ones which, upon accumulating, constitute a life . . . The truth: hardly ever is it provided, although it may be very possible. Lies, lies and lies.]

The matter is larger than the artist himself. Society tells us lies and is not interested in the true reality of our lives. The Vanguardia artist wants to stop being subservient to a controlling system. Whereas the Dadaists wanted to free words, Palacio sought to free his entire narrative from convention. Ultimately, Palacio includes an outright condemnation of traditional writers:

Lo vergonzoso está en que de esas mentiras dicen: te doy un compendio de la vida real, ésto que escribo es la pura y neta verdad; y todos se lo creen. Lo único honrado sería decir: éstas son fantasías, más o menos doradas para que puedas tragártelas con comodidad; o, sencillamente, no dorar la fantasía y dar entretenimiento a lo John Raffles o Sherlock Holmes. ¡Embusteros! ¡Embusteros! (72-73)
[The shamefulness of those lies is that they say: I'm giving you a compendium of real life, this that I write is the pure and absolute truth; and everyone believes it. The only honorable thing would be to say: these are fantasies, more or less coated so that you can swallow them

comfortably; or, simply, to not sugarcoat the fantasies and give them entertainment á la John Raffles or Sherlock Holmes.   Liars! Tricksters!]

The deceit of realist fiction is harmful because it says it is the truth and yet it is not; it generates a vision of a world that tells lies that efficiently control the community. By tapping into the roots of culture and society, only the artist can reveal this deceit: "El arte es el termómetro de la cultura de los pueblos" (Art is the thermometer of the people's culture; 73), states the narrator. With that pronouncement, the Lieutenant's character appears to be lost completely. Soon, however, he returns and interrupts the narrator in order to continue his frustrated story. But as soon as he begins, the structure breaks down again—often mid-sentence—to a white space, thus ending one fragment and beginning another, alternating between the manipulation and control of the text by the narrator and the character's attempt to tell his story.

Unlike a Realist, Palacio makes clear that what he writes is not real. The inspiration of a character makes the collection of fragments possible, while the artist can only attempt to put it into language. Since the artist's attempt at creation is thwarted because he is not a realist or romantic, he is open to new insights and new laws. He has to question Realism because it is the reality of the middle-class, the society he scorns (Ruffinelli 138). Palacio thumbs his nose, like the French Surrealists, at the society which repudiates him. It is a militant stance as a novelist that makes him different from others (Ruffinelli 145).

In this way, the artist's labor-in-process, or contemplation of the work's creation, seems similar to that of philosophers or scientists—a process to encourage thinking. Palacio wants the reader to think; he seeks involvement by making the reader a part of the artistic creation, requiring his participation. For Palacio, everyone should participate in this adventure and help determine its outcome (Flores Jaramillo 59).

The narrator (with whom the artist is identified) functions as much to tell a story as to judge and contemplate it; the narrator directs himself to the characters and to the reader and jokes with them. But Palacio's parody had a very serious intention:

Que podía burlarse del mundo porque sabía burlarse de sí mismo. Que parecía no tomarse en serio la vida justamente porque la tomaba en serio (Flores Jaramillo 18).
[Who could make fun of the world because he knew how to make fun of himself. Who seemed not to take life seriously precisely because he did take it seriously.]

Palacio not only presents a novel in full process of creation, but also his opinions on the various ways of creating a novel (a somewhat quijotesque maneuver). Palacio uses first and third person, interior monologue, free indirect style, and has the characters talk to each other in asides. The resulting discourse on the social and economic problems of his country (Ecuador's financial crisis begins in 1922, followed by the lieutenants' rebellion in 1925) is a Bakhtinian heteroglossia, or alternation of voices, continually changing the reader's perspective. The purpose is not to confuse but to bring attention to numerous social issues the author wanted to denounce, i.e., poverty and the city's homeless:

Sobre todo emocionan los niños, arrojados como trapos; dormidos, con la piel sucia al aire . . . Tu madre te echará a la calle, serás ladrón o prostituta.   De hambre roerás tus propias carnes.   Algún día te acorralará la rabia . . . Después dirán: amor y bondad, ¿Qué amor? ¿Qué bondad? (74)
[Above all the children make one cry, cast aside like rags, asleep {on the street}, their dirty skin exposed to the air . . . Your mother will throw you out on the street, you will be a thief or a prostitute.   In hunger you will gnaw at your own flesh. Someday the rage will corner you . . . Later they will say: love and kindness, What love? What kindness?]

The other character, Lieutenant B, talks to the Lieutenant about a friend of his, Antonio, who was institutionalized because he went crazy. This state of madness is not unlike being a lieutenant, a teacher, a priest, or even a brute, the narrator says, for each one is similar to the other. Like Roberto Arlt, Palacio is showing that the message of a crazy person is a warning that "reason" and tradition—mainstays of his era—cannot provide valid ways out for the character or the novel itself (Fernández 324).[ii]

When the Lieutenant visits the cheaper side of town, populated with prostitutes, the poor, and the homeless, he feels as though he were descending into hell (Lucifer is even mentioned on page 77):

Dentro todo está sucio y emocionante. Hay una verdadera agencia de carnes viejas. Muchas camas y muchas voces. No importa que los vecinos charlen y se rían o que haya borrachos hediondos (76).
[Inside everything is filthy and emotional. There is a true agency of old flesh. Many beds and many voices. It does not matter that the neighbors talk and laugh or that there are smelly drunks.]

He is awaiting a "girl," a sexual experience, and first expects to find a paramour in that part of town. Later in the novel he discovers that a young woman living in his own apartment building is an easy conquest. Her entrance, however, provokes a stereotypical and racist view of the mestizo and Indian:

> Entró la muchacha. Un poco chola y con los pelos gruesos. La carretera de los piojos en la mitad, y con trenzas. Sólo que era exuberante y de boca jugosa (83).
> [The girl walked in. She was a little too much indian with grossly thick hair: a path for fleas in the middle, and with braids. But she was exuberant and had a playful mouth.]

Palacio describes, as the Lieutenant's ultimate conquest, an easy, ignorant, and unbecoming young Indian woman. He pinpoints societal and racial concerns that would later predominate in the Social Realist novel of international recognition (with Icaza's 1934 novel).

As postmodern theorist Patricia Waugh notes, parody is an essential tool of metaliterature in demonstrating artistic style:

> Parody of an earlier literary norm or mode unavoidably lays bare the relations of that norm to its original historical context through its defamiliarizing contextualization within a historical present whose literary and social forms have shifted (Waugh 66).

In his novel *Un hombre muerto a puntapiés*, Palacio parodies Rationalism (and Latin American Positivism) with a character who is a detective and deduces by means of intuition or, "if possible, proof" (Fernández 315). Palacio mocks literary Realism as a combination of conventional norms that become anachronistic in a crucial moment, in his *Novela guillotinada* (Guillotined Novel; 1927). In *Débora*, Palacio parodies the actual development of the novel and its characters.

Débora has three components: (1) the Lieutenant's reminiscences and thoughts interspersed with the narrator's commentary on literature; (2) Lieutenant B's appearance and conversation with the principal character; and (3) more literary notions along with the encounter with a "girl" and the Lieutenant's death. Together, they formulate Palacio's discourse of the need for a new novel alongside the need for change in society. Just as the character is never fully developed, neither is Palacio's plot.

The novel opens with the appearance of what has been inside the artist's head for years, to whom he speaks in the personal form, "tú" (you):

TENIENTE
has sido mi huésped durante años. Hoy te arrojo de mí para que seas la
befa de los unos y la melancolía de los otros.
Muchos se encontrarán en tus ojos como se encuentran en el fondo de
los espejos. . . . ¿Por qué existes? . . . Es verdad que eres inútil. . . .
(Palacio 35)
[LIEUTENANT
you have been my guest for years. Today I throw you out of me so that
you can be the scoff of some and the melancholy of others. Many will
find themselves in your eyes as they find themselves in the depths of
mirrors. . . . Why do you exist? . . .It is true that you are useless. . . .]

The new novel is launched by means of the character, or creative
spirit that has existed within the artist. Some may scoff at the idea of
the character's independence, but the artist indicates he is giving rein to
his character even as he controls his life span. The character,
essentially, is his double:

¿Y cómo te dejo, Teniente? Ya arrancado de mí volitivamente, tengo
prisa por la pérdida. Ante una amenaza definitiva e indispensable,
surge la espera de la amenaza, y es tan fuerte como la espera de la
novia. Quiero verte salido de mí. . . . Ir, cogidos de los brazos, atento al
desarrollo de lo casual. Hacer el ridículo, lo profundamente ridículo,
que hace sonreír al dómine, y que congestionado dirá, "Pero qué es
esto? Este hombre está loco." Ve, alargando mi brazo y con el
indicador estirado (37).
[And how shall I leave you, Lieutenant? Now yanked out of me
volitionally, I am in a hurry for the loss. Before a definitive and
indispensable threat, surges the wait for the threat, and it is as strong as
the wait for the loved one. I want to see you removed from me. . . . To
go, arm in arm, attentive to the development of casual things. To be
ridiculous, profoundly ridiculous, enough to make the teacher smile,
who, congested, will say: "But, what is this? This man is crazy." Go
now, stretching my arm with the indicator pointing.]

This is a powerful statement of release of artistic spirit (an
interesting comparison to the biblical Moses stretching his rod, with
God's power, over the Red Sea). From this point, the character begins
his own journey, greeting a captain and saluting rigidly, which causes
the narrator to muse for several pages on his character's good training
and personal history. The narrator expresses worry about the
experiences the Lieutenant has not had (as though he were his child):

Es preciso entrar en las suposiciones, buscando el artificio, y dar al
Teniente lo que no tuvo, la prima de las novelas y también de la vida,
que trae fresco olor de membrillo. Pero la historia no estará aquí: se la

ha de buscar en el índice de alguna novela romántica y así tendremos que unas manos blancas acariciaron unos cabellos rubios y que el propietario de estos cabellos sentía crecer la malicia desde el cuero cabelludo, malicia soñolienta. Este supuesto recuerdo que debe estar en los arcones de cada hombre, hace suspirar al Teniente. . . . (41-42).
[lit is necessary to suppose, seek artificial things, and give the Lieutenant what he did not have, the womanly essence of novels and also of life, that brings a fresh smell of quince. But that history is not here; it must be sought in the index of some romantic novel and then we will have that some white hands caressed some blonde hair and that the owner of that hair felt some malice arise from her very scalp, a lazy malice. This supposed memory which should be in every man's deepest memories, makes the Lieutenant sigh. . . .]

Palacio makes sentimentality seem foolish: the Lieutenant's sighs upon thinking of a woman and intimacy with her. But he also sighs when he thinks about his unmatched socks and dirty shoes. The narrator calls him "stupid" (42), perhaps because Palacio knew that his undeveloped character and novel would be considered so by literary critics. Then he intervenes in the plot and discusses the desired quality of an artistic creation. He notices that the Lieutenant is lost in thoughts of a woman he once knew. So the narrator uses that opportunity to appropriate the woman to explain his own artistic frustrations:

La intimidad está apaciblemente llena del anhelo de la mujer. Con ellas, viene el "¿para qué?" o la indiferencia, o el descuido, o el considerarlas, a pesar de que haya llegado el momento propicio, lejanas aun dentro de su proximidad.. . . Esta es la lección del amor (47).
[Intimacy is peacefully full of wishing for the woman of one's dreams. But with {the women} comes a feeling of "what for?", or indifference, or carelessness, or contemplating them; although the propitious moment has come, they are far away even within their nearness. . . . This is the lesson of love.]

The woman, as muse, is pursued with desire and longing. But this endeavor only brings greater frustration when her affection or inspiration does not arrive, and the artist feels empty—in other words, she can be there, and yet feel far away. Pablo Palacio, like Arqueles Vela and Roberto Arlt, voices the frustration he knows he will encounter as he attempts to create a new novel.

When the Lieutenant finds some money in the street, the narrator analyzes his reaction. The Lieutenant estimates how much money it would take to live the "good life," and the narrator reflects on the character's reflections. The Lieutenant's logic is like a "text" and the narrator/author gently creates puns based on rationalistic thought and the realist novel (51). Palacio uses figures and calculations (a strategy of the Futurists) to show the impact of numbers on human life—like money—which could ease the Lieutenant's agony over dirty shoes and empty pockets. His characters reflect a problem for the middle class of his day, who were caught between idealism (or fantasy) and sordid reality (Corral 353). New ideologies and a taste of capitalism in the 1920s seemed to only worsen the situation of the poor.

Palacio's Peruvian contemporary, José Carlos Mariátegui (1895-1930), a political leader and literary critic who launched the influential journal, *Amauta*, in 1926, noted that artists of the period were often more likely to be concerned with a critique of the middle class than inventing a new style:

> El sentido revolucionario de las escuelas o tendencias contemporáneas no está en la creación de una técnica nueva. No está tampoco en la destrucción de la técnica vieja. Está en el repudio, en el desahucio, en la befa del absoluto burgués (Corral 355).
> [The revolutionary sense of the contemporary schools or tendencies is not in the creation of a new technique. Nor is it in the destruction of the old technique. It is in the repudiation, in the dispossesion, in scoffing the absolute member of the bourgeosie.]

While Palacio often censures society, he seems to defy Mariátegui's statement by doing much more than simply repudiating the rising middle class. He strove to express the artist's thoughts in the process of creating the novel, an endeavor that can take on new methods, just as new technological methods were changing the way society worked.

The second component of *Débora* includes specific information relating to where the Lieutenant is and goes (to the neighborhoods of San Marcos, La Ronda, the lower-class section, to his home, and to the Casino). In his journey around the city, this character examines the old and the traditional, as suggested by a description of a church and the histories of neighborhoods. The artist is perusing the traditional for guidance. The next morning the Lieutenant in a positive spirit takes a deep breath, and prepares to enjoy a beautiful day. Hands in his pockets, an idea occurrs to him: a military person should not walk around with his hands in his pockets, so he removes them (59). Palacio's narrator insists that these aspects are important in the development of a character, apparently tongue-in-cheek, such as the following scene:

> Abundancia naturalista: se hurgó las narices con el dedo meñique. Es un detalle nimio; pero lo primero es la observación (59).

[Naturalist abundance: He blew his nostrils with his little finger. It is a fastidious detail, but what is important is observation.]

This habit is like that of cutting his toenails in bed one morning (60)—all parodies of realist and naturalist novels which were popular for several decades in Latin America. The observation of details, even if not pretty, was sought for its supposed portrayal of real life. Following this description, the Lieutenant walks outside and encounters Lieutenant B:

--Hola, Teniente B.
. . . El Teniente B es un amigo de nuestro Teniente.
Se dieron las manos.
--¿Qué tal?
--¿Qué tal?
--¿Qué es de la vida?
--Bien, ¿y tú?
Etc.
--Oye lo que me pasa.
--¿ ?
--Ayer estuve con ella.
--¿Sí? Cuenta. (59).
[Hello, Lieutenant B.
. . . The Lieutenant B is a friend of our Lieutenant.
They shook hands.
How're you doing?
How are you doing?
How is life treating you?
Fine, and you?
Etc.
Hey, listen to what's happening to me.
??
His eyes looked like they were having a good time.
Yesterday I was with her.
Really? Do tell.]

Most of this dialogue is actually descriptive information for the reader, for example, of what the Lieutenant's friend, Lieutenant B's, eyes looked like. Also, the principal character is referred to as "our" Lieutenant, assuring the reader that he is an integral part of the story. At this point the narrator breaks the dialogue noting that he should provide an update about "her."Lieutenant's B's paramour is portrayed as an ephemereal, romantic figure and, until the final description of the (principal) Lieutenant's Indian "girl," she is the only woman actually described in the novel. But only her laugh, ankles, and shoes are revealed. More important seems to be who and why she marries:

Ella se casó con un abogado de color. Buen negocio. Un cualquiera, una cualquiera; pero él era jurisconsulto. Por supuesto, se da como sentado la belleza de ella . . . (60).
[She married a lawyer of color. Good business. A commoner, a (woman) commoner; but he was a jurisconsult. Of course, it is a given that she was beautiful. . . .]

This is a satire of the bourgeois idea of business, money, and advancement, with the romantic twist (probably played out in radio soap operas, films, and stories of Palacio's day) of a beautiful woman able to marry a financially-suited man. In this case, however, the man also represents a minority, a person "of color." Obviously, it was helpful for him to marry a beautiful (white?) woman. The scene is not only a parody of the romantic novel but also, again, a denunciation of society's prejudices.

Lieutenant B continues his story, saying that yesterday he was summoned to his lover's house because her husband was away. His story builds around their ecstatic liaison until, naturally, someone knocks at the door. Assuming it is her husband, Lieutenant B hides; she opens the door, and people are heard talking while he lies under a sofa. As she returns to the room where he is hiding, he sees only her ankles and does not recognize her at first. The narrator's voice describes the incident and their resumed lovemaking. Lieutenant B's account ends without any commentary from the Lieutenant. A false build-up toward an assumed occurrence is a continuing motif in the novel.

Halfway into the 55-page novel, the two lieutenants decide to go out on the town. The section is titled "La Ronda" (The Outing; also an old street in colonial Quito), and the narrator notes that upon reading that title, people will imagine a lovely Spanish caper with serenades of guitars and drunken confessions; instead, the narrator criticizes the demise of the old neighborhoods as modernization takes over the city. He even uses the word "suburb" (66) as he goes on and on about the "emotion" one could feel. The only action of this anecdote, however, involves the lieutenants having dinner in a restaurant; while there, Lieutenant B tells the Lieutenant about their friend Antonio, who is currently in a "mad" state, in an asylum. The narrator interrupts their chat because he remembers a personal letter the Lieutenant received recently, and seems to be sharing it with the reader without the Lieutenant's knowledge. Upon a critique of the letter's style, this fragment ends abruptly. Palacio's habit of stopping and starting accounts, building up to a scene that becomes nothing at all, increases tension for the reader, who must create the plot himself.

As the Lieutenant walks the dark and empty streets with his hands in his pockets again, the narrator launches into a tirade about the ineffectiveness of the realist novel (72-73). The Lieutenant stops abruptly when he remembers a certain adobe stairway, which leads down to a black door, where he had discovered "her" before. Crime, filth, and shame seem to lurk behind that door, but it is the kind of place where neighbors never complain, even about smelly drunks. It is almost like hell. This scene is a parody of Naturalism, with its ugly, realistic details.

The Lieutenant abruptly leaves this place, however, and, while walking, hears footsteps behind him. He stops, but does not see anyone, and continues walking. "Otros pasos, entonces tuvo miedo" (A few more steps, then he felt afraid; 78). Even though he is intensely cold, he continues to feel stronger, and later he wonders why he was afraid. He begins to think about going home, where the sheets will be cold, and where his wish for a woman will not be fulfilled:

> Bueno, después de todo, en resumen, se ha hablado de la espera de la mujer. No vendrá nunca la mujer única, que conviene a nuestros intereses, que existe y que no sabemos dónde está (79).
> [Well, after all, in summary, the wait for the woman has been mentioned. The one and only woman will never come, the one that fits our interests, that exists and that we do not know where to find.]

Essentially, the narrator is revealing that nothing will happen in this novel; similarly, even though the Lieutenant has a hope, it will not be fulfilled. Palacio is metaphorically expressing hope for the perfect novel or artistic creation, which could actually exist somewhere. The lonely evening continues as the narration launches into an episode called "Tentativa de Seducción" (Attempt at Seduction). The false buildup (the footsteps behind him) to this fragment alludes to a possible crime, which is an imitation of the detective novel; the words "tentativa de delito" are common in the Spanish language, meaning attempt to commit a crime. The niece of his landlady, budding with puberty, whom the Lieutenant has often greeted on the porch, turns red when she sees him. The "tentativa" (attempt or suggestion) becomes a plan (81). His carnal needs recognized in the lower side of town have helped him see a series of possibilities with each of the women (although no others are described) he desires, of whom the present one seems to be the easiest to conquer (81). Here, the idea of "women" stands for the various possibilities for novels in the artist's head, of which one is apparently chosen and explored for a reason as inexplicable as the Lieutenant's reasons for choosing the girl:

Facilidades: ausencia de la tía; disponibilidad de ella porque de su examen externo se comprende bien claro que es boba. Es boba, es boba, es boba. A la casa no va nadie (82).
[Conveniences: the aunt's absence; {the girl's} availability because an external examination reveals that she is an idiot. She's an idiot, an idiot, an idiot. And no one goes to their home.]

When the plan is set, the Lieutenant feels like a conquerer. But several days go by before he sees her, because he was lazy, or he had to go out on the town, or to the movies, or his shoes were dirty, or he did not feel like shaving (82). Finally, he cleans his fingernails, freshens his mouth with chewing gum, and pays her a visit. He describes her as a gangly, ugly, chatty teenager. He kisses her hand and notices that her face turns red. He thinks this must be a joy for her; then he leaves. The narrator notes that the Lieutenant always wears spurs, which make a noise when he walks. This perplexing detail creates an odd and abrupt break in the plot line. Time passes. The next visit to the teenager is more intimate. The Lieutenant moves his chair closer and rubs against her flabby arms. When she does not move her arm he starts to rub her neck. When he asks for a kiss on the mouth, she first says no, but then acquiesces.

The narrator states only that the third visit is even more successful, and the anecdote ends. The reader is left with the idea that this is the long-awaited love affair for the Lieutenant (and that the artist has finally connected with his muse). But the lack of detail on his third visit terminates the idea even as the Lieutenant's life ends in the following, and final, fragment. Palacio's experimentation with a character and the novel seem futile at first. According to Realism, a presentation of all the "facts" should lead to verisimilitude. And in Positivism, specific details on the "how" are more important than the "why." Palacio shows the ineptitude of the conventional novel with realist and romantic strategies. The new novel must do something more than follow a romantic plot or seek verity in representation (Fernández 299). Realism and the conventional novel are no longer relevant in the twentieth century, especially when many people live in poverty and political distress.

The final page of *Débora* is titled "Teniente," and begins by telling of the Lieutenant's recent death, again in personal "tú" form as in the opening. His death, the narrator says, is apparently from a paper cut: a vertical cut to the smooth dangling of the facts (90). This death is similar to Arqueles Vela's murder of a mannequin; each a parody of the popular detective novel. The narrator then observes the night and thinks of his unattainable woman/muse:

Débora está demasiado lejos y por eso es una magnolia. Habríamos ido
a verla. Débora: bailarina yanquilandesa. Dos ojos azules. Sabía dar
a los brazos flexibilidades de cuellos de garza. Imagino que tiene un
lejano sabor de miel (90).
[Deborah is much too far away and that is why she is a magnolia. We
would have gone to see her.Deborah: yankeeland dancer. Two blue
eyes. She knew how to gingerly move her arms like a crane's neck. I
imagine that she has a faraway taste of honey.]

   This meditation on the woman desired by the Lieutenant (a
"Deborah" is never mentioned by him) is an expression of the
narrator/author's idea and hope for artistic inspiration. But the artist is
not moved by traditional influences. Deborah is a dancer and a
"yankee," an elusive spirit from the most powerful country in the
hemisphere (which also controls Ecuador's economy). The crane's
neck—a semblance of art and also of a question mark—could be a
replacement for the Latin American Modernistas' perpetual swan,
whose neck needed to be twisted according to one poet critiquing
Modernismo. Foreign inspiration is considered sweeter, Palacio notes
with an allusion to honey. But the foreign inspiration does not arrive.
His character never even meets "her." A dependence on foreign
influences or traditional formulas will not bring about the new novel.
   On the final page of Palacio's novel, he pulls together his parallel
points of the denunciation of his generation's social dilemma, and the
condemnation of traditional narrative structure preferred by the
bourgeosie. In parody form, he concludes by promising to retain the
bourgeosie's need for tradition, directing himself to the Lieutenant, but
in essence, to his own generation:

   Y por temor a corromper ese recuerdo guardo tu ridículo yo. Todos los
   hombres guardarán un momento su yo para paladear el lejano sabor de
   Débora, la que luchará cada vez más desmayadamente y a más largos
   intérvalos, como un muelle que va perdiendo fuerza. En este momento
   inicial y final suprimo las minucias y difumino los contornos d eu ns u
   a v ec o l o rb l a n c o(sic; 90).
   [And in fear of corrupting that memory, I will keep your ridiculousness
   myself. All men will keep themselves for a moment in order to taste
   that faraway flavor of Deborah, who will struggle each time more
   languidly and for longer intervals, like a pier that is losing hold. In this
   initial and final moment I suppress the minutiae and perplex the outline
   o fas o f tw h i t ec o l o r (sic).]

   The Modernistas made the color "white" (for virginal purity)
famous in their poetry, using it to show the inspiration they needed to
reach artistic creation. The sexual act was a metaphor for the union of

inspiration (white, virginal purity) with the artistic spirit. The idea was used so frequently by male poets that the late Modernista poet Delmira Agustini mockingly titled a poem "Blanca que me quieres blanca" (White that you want me white). Palacio does more than poke fun at the Modernistas' use of white, he called attention to it as a blank space—empty and ready for new creation. Palacio showed the artist's desire for guidance by using the name of a biblical prophetess. Deborah, as a muse, led the artist to the soft white color that is only apparent after "suppressing" the outlines and minutiae of tradition.

The artist's presence is a constant in *Débora*, he has the power and control over the writing. The narrator's manipulation—the Lieutenant cannot construct himself, and the narrator abruptly interrupts the conversation between the two lieutenants—of the absence of information and the constant changes in person or voice, destabilizes a conventional view of the world. Palacio wanted to show the artist's power to supplant the conventional and, similar to Mario Vargas Llosa's idea, the act of devouring to replace, as in Brazilian anthropomorphy. Nothing is sure in Palacio's novel and plot is even less important. This instability is essential to his discourse; after all, the story is about the novel, not about the Lieutenant:

> Aunque también el amigo nos distrae y es causa de una fuga concentrativa, perdemos el hilo de lo que obstinadamente teníamos en el cerebro, importante o estúpido, pero obsesionante (55).
> [Although also the friend distracts us and is the cause of an escape in concentration, we lose the point of what we obstinately had in mind, important or stupid, but obsessive.]

The traditional novel has been mimicked, parodied and, finally, put to rest as useless, to make way for the new novel, in which the character and even the reader have key parts to play (Hutcheon 253).

Débora's structure is like a puzzle: it is a sequence of moments joined by the sole logic of fright or desolation; a grouping of strange meditations; a coupling of the abstract and concrete (Fernández 319-320). If the story is about a Lieutenant with an unsatisfied wish, to whom nothing of consequence happens before death, then the structure coincides with the plot. The lack of structure and an empty plot filled with pessimism and social censure renders an empty novel. But Palacio's novel consists of much more than nothingness: His principal character, the pathetic, retrospective, sentimental Lieutenant, dies the death of the conventional novel so that in this "initial and final moment" (Palacio 90) a new creation comes into being.

The world of the novel is a verbal construction. Since the two lieutenants do not even have names, only their actions, however few, are important. The frustrations, plans, and pursuit of a woman is a metaphor for the artist's hope and pursuit of creation; these frustrations also express the specific socio-historical moment of Palacio's generation:. . . Showing us how literary fiction creates its imaginary worlds . . . helps us to understand how the reality we live day by day is similarly constructed, similarly "written" (Waugh 18).

Palacio's discourse is an explanation of possibility and renewal in life, society, and art. The reader is offered two possibilities: (1) the revelation of what is within his own conscience (in other words, that the reader and the author are a part of the internal world he is articulating); and (2) an outside, external point of view of the artist's conscience at work, as though someone were describing it (Jitrik 164). Thus, it is difficult for the reader to maintain distance, and, if he does, the reader still sees himself through the external viewpoint of the development and critique of narrative and society.

In his definitive study on the new novel, *Ideas sobre el teatro y la novela* (Ideas on Theater and the Novel; 1925), José Ortega y Gasset stated that if art is a deformation of reality and therefore incompatible with it, it removes the reader from the cares of everyday life. His intention was to warn the young, modern writer against producing art that does not match, or fit, the new era. Palacio does not construct his art to be incomprehensible, but to portray a novel-in-the-making, and the *necessity* of new artistic creation. Narrative fiction cannot be done in the same manner the romantic or realist novels were constructed, just as Miguel de Cervantes could not and did not construct a novel based on the conventional novels of his day. Cervantes' unusual footnotes, supposed errors, and misleading information in *Don Quijote* (1605) served as a base for criticism of the conventional novel, and parodied the extremely popular *novelas de caballerías* (novels about knights and their quests for honor). Palacio is using abstractions, not to make art less understood but, much like his contemporaries in other Latin American, North American and European countries, to revise the novel. In this, he is as effective as Gustave Flaubert or James Joyce in portraying a reality that is more real and up-to-date than Realism itself (Pareja Diez Canseco 101).

The French writer Jean Giraudoux (1882-1944) influenced Hispanic writers, according to Susan Nagel, and was included by Ortega y Gasset in his list of writers who were too abstract. Giraudoux wrote metafictional prose in the 1920s that required the reader to use his own imagination and participate in the novel (Nagel 78). This did not imply a rejection of reality, or even of universality as Ortega y Gasset feared (76); instead, Giraudoux simply does away with traditional components like omniscient author and the elaborately contrived plot. He constantly reminds the reader to reflect upon the novel by revealing its conventions and disposing of them. Palacio's reader similarly sees traditional fiction die as Palacio's romantic character dies. Giraudoux, and many Latin American Vanguardia writers, invited the reader to participate in the creative process (14); the modern world demanded that writers adapt to discoveries in science and philosophy.

Ortega y Gasset did not understand that many modern writers wanted to trust their readers' imaginations by having the readers complete the images in their novels. He and other critics paid no attention to the subtleties of parody and irony in these writers' visions, suggesting instead an appreciation of style without substance. Like Giraudoux's fiction, Palacio's novels are about art, but ultimately about the moral, philosophical, and social problems of mankind (29). Just as Nagel's book demonstrates Giraudoux's subtle criticism of art and society that few of his contemporary critics understood, so Palacio's work can be rediscovered for its subtleties in the postmodern era, and consequently, his work's status as precursor to the *new* Latin American novel.

---

[i] The "Fernández" quoted in this chapter is María del Carmen Fernández, not "Bustos Fernández," or "Fernández Retamar."

[ii] Some of Palacio's peers and other critics have noted his madness later in his life and the fact he died in an insane asylum as perhaps connected to his way of producing his novel. Despite that general possibility, it would seem more likely that his illness could have resulted from physical and emotional factors, such as his mother's death, his father's abandonment, and the following incident, all occurring when he was three years old: A maid took him with her to wash clothes in a river, he fell in and was washed miles and miles downstream, hit his head, and received seventeen stitches; it was amazing that he lived. It does not seem likely his artistic genius is at all related to his madness (Carrión 33).

CHAPTER FIVE

NOSTALGIA FOR THE FUTURE IN PERU

The arrival of *Vanguardia* in Peru led to a virtual metaphor factory among Peruvian intellectuals in a literary community that seemed to burst in its attempts to create a new language (Anderson Imbert 200). César Vallejo (1892-1938), Peru's most famous citizen of this period and an initiator of Vanguardia poetry in Latin America, and other artists created poetry and prose with an eye to be pure, new, different, and Peruvian. Like Vallejo, some also sought to represent the chaos of their rapidly-changing era through politically-committed verse. Vallejo arrived in Lima in 1917 and published *Los heraldos negros* in 1919. *Trilce*, published in 1922, was partially based on his years in jail as a political prisoner. These books, especially the latter, were openly critical of Determinism and the Modernista tradition.

With the exception of Brazil, Peru's Vanguardia was more unified and had more nationalistic orientation than other Latin American countries, which identified primarily with specific urban areas. Peru's first renovative literary stirrings occurred before the 1920s (as in Brazil) in futurist poems and in journals such as *La Tea* (1917-19), published by the "Bohemia literaria" group in Puno, and *La Semana* (1918-23), published in Arequipa (Forster 138). Vallejo's poetry is the most obvious example of Peru's early Vanguardia production; a more intense period began in 1924 with the first definitively avant-garde journal, *Flechas*, which published four issues that year. Two subsequent journals, *Boletín Titikaka*, published in Puno, and *Amauta*, published in Lima (both 1926-1930), helped sustain an examination of developments in the arts, including national, international, and American (the continent) issues (the Rodó philosophy, vis-a-vis indigenous questions). After Vallejo, Martín Adán (née Rafael de la Fuente Benavides, 1908-1984) has recently begun to receive attention as a significant figure of the 1920s.

Born 16 years after Vallejo, Adán began publishing poetry as a teenager and started a novel when he was 18 years old. Matched by few when he turned to prose, his short novel, *La casa de cartón* (1928;

The Cardboard House, 1990), published when Adán was 20 years old, is the outstanding piece of Vanguardia narrative of the 1920s in Peru. It contains repeated descriptions of smells and sounds, elaborated in short sentences and paragraphs, not unlike Arqueles Vela's prose. Adán is seen as a rarity who began his craft by reworking old Spanish style—sonnets, stanzas, romantic verse—to include neologisms (newly invented words), giddy metaphors, and magical lyricism. He called his sonnets "anti-sonnets" (Anderson Imbert 201).   This early experimentation in poetry, and his use of irony, all enhance Adán's prose.

Peru in the 1920s was similar to Ecuador: it was attempting to modernize and improve its economy while recovering from wars and political destabilization. Although this region was a major source of wealth for the Spanish during the colonial period, i.e., the silver mines of Potosí in Upper Peru (now Bolivia) and other precious metals found later in Peru, these sources had all but disappeared after Independence. The capital, Lima, called the City of Kings, was an important city for the Spanish, who founded the University of San Marcos and built an impressive cathedral in the early 1550s. The metropolis was rivaled only by Mexico City (Skidmore 189). By 1820, Lima's importance had faded for two reasons: Peru had separated from former Upper Peru, and Buenos Aires had become a major trade center. The stuggle for independence left Peru's principal port, Callao, in ruins, and the fledgling government began acquiring foreign debt as did many small Latin American countries. However, Peru found another product that brought it into the twentieth century: first discovered in the 1830s, the boom in *guano* (fertilizer) came in the 1840s.[i] As demand increased in European countries, guano exports fell into the hands of foreigners, although the Peruvian government leased exploitation rights.   The rights to guano sales created political struggles for years.

One of Peru's impressive presidents, Ramón Castilla, achieved power through armed struggles in 1844-45 and 1855-1862. A poorly educated *mestizo*, he seemed to favor the lower classes. Due to his views on national responsiblity and economic development, he decreed the end of the Indian (indigenous) tribute and immediate emancipation of slaves; in his second term, he improved public education, supported military professionalization, and presided over assemblies that produced two constitutions, a federalist document and a centralized charter (Skidmore 193). He also pressed for continental unity that would ensure greater respect for South American republics. Castilla's philosophy and actions are noted because several presidents of the nineteenth century seemed interested primarily in power for personal gain.

Peru's greatest loss in the nineteenth century was the disastrous War of the Pacific (1879-1883) with Chile, in which Peru was forced to give precious nitrate areas to its southern neighbor. In 1895, a bloody civil war installed the progressive *Civilista* party, which ruled through various presidents and dictators for more than two decades. Despite the Civilistas' efforts to expand education, the country was about ninety percent illiterate and social mobility had only fractionally increased by 1919, when the first major workers' strike occurred in Peru. Workers had been hurt by the depression at the end of World War I, socialist and workers' parties began preaching the doctrine of class struggle, and industrial labor became a force to be reckoned with. Augusto Leguía, a former one-term president, took over in 1919 and ruled as dictator until 1930 (Franco 1967, 82). Cited in *La casa de cartón*, he worked on economic development, transportation and public works projects, but the country's social situation, work opportunities, and education scarcely improved during his tenure.

As the guano economy declined, Peru began to depend on its sugar and cotton exports, as well as mining. Wool from the Andes mountains accounted for as much as ten percent of Peru's exports between 1918-1920, after which the market collapsed. Copper was the most important mineral product in the second decade, and petroleum production began after World War I. By 1930 oil comprised 30 percent of Peru's total exports. Leguía's economic policy was to promote an export-import model of growth, but the post-war slowdown in trade reduced the amount of capital available for investment; hence Leguía encouraged domestic investment, for example, in public works. When the terms of trade began leading to the depreciation of the nation's currency, however, Perú's capitalist elite expressed alarm. In 1922 the Central Bank sold off a large share of gold and foreign reserves, and in the mid-1920s a large-scale loan maintained a high exchange rate for the Peruvian monetary system. Intellectuals began to denounce the false prosperity of guano sales and the reliance on foreign exports; and they called for resistance to yankee imperialism, which they considered the controlling force over the Peruvian economy (Skidmore 192).

Intellectual communities during the first two decades of the century, consisting of a small population of writers and fewer than two thousand university students and their professors, sought, in their writings, to explain political and economic strife. The most reknowned intellectual was Manuel González Prada (1848-1918), who wanted to destroy all old institutions and reconstruct society based on the culture of the indigenous masses (Tamayo Vargas 188). González Prada's immediate influence was small, but he would be a posthumous prophet for future reform leaders. (Argentina's university reform movement of

1918 had spread to Lima, where students also supported workers in the general strike of 1919). At the end of World War I, modernization had not yet penetrated Peru's hinterlands; its growth was to prove agonizingly slow for Peru's economy, and a disaster for the disenfranchised population. It was only after 1930 that modernization, political progress, and reforms made headway in Peru.

González Prada's principal disciples, José Carlos Mariátegui (1895-1930) and Víctor Raúl Haya de la Torre (1895-1979; the latter exiled in 1922 for opposition to Leguía's dictatorial rule), helped launch the American Popular Revolutionary Alliance (APRA) in 1924. This Marxist political force espoused an anti-imperialist and generally anticapitalist doctrine.   Peruvian conservatives called APRA communist, but communists also denounced APRA, fearing a leftist challenge to their own party. Supporters of APRA's philosophy and subsequent pressure for change, however, came from a wide range of society—intellectuals and students, labor leaders, workers, and even some members of the middle class. By the 1930s, goals inspired by APRA penetrated Peruvian society as well as literature. Martín Adán would be one of the earliest to reflect societal unrest and technological change in prose fiction in Peru.

Haya de la Torre's cry against imperialist intervention was strongest. In the 1930s, he returned to Peru and ran for political office as an APRA candidate. Also a proponent of the APRA philosophy, Mariátegui founded the Socialist Party in 1929. Although he died in 1930 without seeing the fruits of his political work, Mariátegui had two great intellectual achievements: (1) he was one of the first in Latin American critical writing to tackle the problem of incorporating the Indian into literature, and (2) he launched the influential journal *Amauta* (Lima, 1926-1930), a wide-ranging review of art and politics which published articles by and about Latin American intellectuals and innovative artists (Franco 1967, 83).

Amauta would be the avenue for Adán's first publication—fragments of his prose which would later become a part of *La casa de cartón*. Published as a novel in 1928, it then remained out of print for thirty years until publisher Juan Mejía Baca released it again in 1958; third and fourth editions followed in 1961 and 1971 (Kinsella 32), and included forewords by Peruvian critic Luis Alberto Sánchez (1900-1988) and Mariátegui. In 1990, Katherine Silver published an English version of the novel, *The Cardboard House*, with a short introduction explaining that she worked image by image rather than word by word in her translation, in order to savor each sight, smell, or flight of fancy evoked by the language.[ii]

Silver notes in her introduction that one critic called Adán's novel "a long prose poem that always returns to the same place, to a particular memory," and that Mario Vargas Llosa called it "a poetic, sensual, intuitive, nonrational testimony of exterior reality" (viii). Adán was not only a poet, but also a staunch member of his Vanguardia generation which sought linguistic adventure; in addition to this first novel, he published *La rosa de la espinela* (The Rose of the Stanza) in 1939. As Silver indicates, Adán is highly respected for his poetry in Latin America. She quotes from a fragment in *La casa de cartón* titled "Underwood Poems," which is supposed to have been written by the narrator's alter-ego, Ramón. Silver uses Adán's own verse to seek the intention of his writing in prose:

> I am not wholly convinced of my own inhumanity: I do not wish to be like others. I do not want to be happy with permission of the police . . . The world is insufficient for me (viii).

Adán foresaw the need for a new prose in the twentieth century. His discourse is based on the shifting forces of life that seldom remain the same except in memory, hence, the cardboard house. He documents the tangible and intangible realities of a coastal village, Barranco, while dealing with global conditions of change and modernization that destroy human qualities for the sake of growth and production. While the novel is critical of the middle-class society of Lima, it is also a tender portrait of a Peruvian landscape. The narrator alternates between morose and fond memories, and the narrative is somewhat expressionistic for its extreme subjectivity and individualism. Through images, Adán shows that while the old is lost, it can be remade a better reality. He renounced traditional narrative to show how the novel could modernize and art could become new (Higgins 292). The village is a metaphor for his art and his art a metaphor for Peruvian life.

More than nostalgia for the old days of Barranco, his descriptions illuminated the old and traditional that "will never be" again. Adán used memories and subconscious observations as images, and the result was his own sensorial, intuitive, non-rational, poetic testimony of an exterior reality in contrast to the traditional Realism of a folkloric Peru (Aguilar Mora 52). Adán's novel is more than lyrical narrative; it is an avant-garde art representation of socio-political conditions, of the traditional novel, and of the impact of Freudianism or psychological impulses on artistic creation. Like Pablo Palacio, Adán documents the making of a novel: he cites and critiques modern and traditional writers, poking fun at conventional rules and structure as he writes his own kind of novel. Similarly to Arqueles Vela, Roberto Arlt, and Pablo Palacio, Adán shows that life's shifting forces of political change and modernization have a correlative in the need for modernization in prose.

La casa de cartón presents the impressions, sensations, and emotions of Barranco, a small village near the Pacific cliffs and 10 minutes from Lima; it is based on the memories of the narrator's adolescent vacations with his family. Adán stakes a claim in his prose for that world of the coastal village, now rapidly changing with economic and tourist invasions. Although there are sharp comments in the novel about a *gringa* (English/Anglo woman) photographer, an older German man, and a *gringo* (U.S. American) travel agent, the plot consists mainly of the narrator's obsession for the loss of his childhood friend Ramón. The narrator addresses a personal "you", usually Ramón, as he recalls their experiences and Ramón's erotic adventures, including his relationship with his girlfriend, Catita. Ramón died young and now the narrator has only memories, just as Peru's first century as an independent nation is a memory as it enters the international world economy. The name "Ramón" coincides perfectly with President Ramón Castilla, and thus, represents both the ahievements and the lost innocence of a previous era. The narrator also has a relationship with Catita and at times addresses her as "you" as well. As the novel develops, in non sequitur short chapters, Ramón and Catita take on the roles of muses.

There are no chapters in this novel of approximately one hundred pages; forty fragments of memories and images make up the text. Surrealistic techniques such as the absence of linear time, the blurring of identities, and an emphasis on the irrational provide for the esthetic series of metaphors. In addition, irony and humor abound in the descriptions, making the purpose of the prose seem only to exalt Barranco:

> Las tardes eran blancas en invierno, y en verano, de un oro rojizo . . .
> Pero en marzo hubo un lunes con la tarde rosa . . . y allí todo el mundo
> se enterneció con la tarde rosa (Adán 43).
> Afternoons were white in winter, and in summer, a reddish gold . . .
> But in March there was a Monday with a pink afternoon . . . and
> everybody was deeply moved by the pink afternoon (Silver 44).

The state of narrative fiction merges with the state of Barranco, a microcosm of Peru, and its/their precarious conditions in a new century where technology and war threaten their very existence:

El cielo, afiliado al vanguardismo, hace de su blancura pulverulenta, nubes redondadas de todos los colores que unas veces parecen pelotas alemanas . . . (42).
Out of its dusty whiteness, the sky—affiliated with the vanguard—creates round, multicolored clouds that at times look like German balls . . . (42).

The reference to "German" is interesting for its correlation to recent technology; the toy ball may have been an inflated one, similar to the world-famous German dirigibles of this era. The artist realizes that his meditation on present life and society will result in an avant-garde creation. In the following paragraph, a melancholic tone pinpoints achievements—technological or human—that only result in the end of the world:

¡Ay del que realiza su deseo! . . . (63)
El mundo está prieto, chico, terroso, como acabado de cosechar en no sé qué infinitud agrícola (42).
Parecía que todo iba a derrumbarse . . . (45).
[Un hombre] . . . al filo de un malecón sin baranda. Quizá todo no es sino elementos esenciales, fechas fisonómicas, cruces y mayúsculas, taquigrafía de observador viandante . . . (47).
Woe to the one that realizes his desire! . . . (71).
The world is little, dark, gritty, as if just harvested in some unknown agricultural infinity. (42).
Everything seemed on the verge of collapse . . . (47).
[A man is at] the edge of the promenade without a railing. Perhaps everything is nothing but the essential elements, physiognomic dates, crosses and capital letters, the shorthand of a wayfaring observer . . . (49).

These words are also a commentary on the frustrations of the creative act: A new harvest, or a novel, is dark, gritty, essentially newborn, and precarious; it could easily collapse or fall off the edge as the author goes about collecting the essential elements to construct the text.

Adán does not look for stable signifiers in his fiction; instead, his scenes run on incessantly as though subconsciously searching throughout its discourse (Elmore 76). European narrative after the turn of the century and preceding World War I sought to interweave reality and imagination, or science and fiction, in order to explain the creative process. But the following generation found science-fiction and popular fiction such as the detective story unable to demonstrate the creative dynamic; instead, they used technology:

> The machine doesn't build, it destroys, it un-builds, it deconstructs at birth the machinery of myth-making . . . Equally, the myth of childhood innocence, the Romantic search for creativity in naivety, is rendered momentarily inoperative by a rapid allusion to a metaphorised experience of the machine: the signifier carburetor, for an emphatic moment, supersedes the signifier 'enfant' (Mathews 128-129).

As this critic explains, the Romantic and post-Romantic artist's representation had to be superseded by a new format, even a new creativity. Latin American artists, primarily residing in urban centers, explored new paths for their fiction that depicted the impact of modern technology. While Vela's narrative was more specifically analogous to technological deconstruction, Adán's narrative oscillates between excitement and anxiety about the impact of technology. It has a "sense of development absolutely disrupted, and of coherence fragmented, gloriously, irredeemably" (Mathews 126)—a central motif of both European and Latin American avant-garde art in the early decades of this century.

In Adán's novel, fear and despair about the creative act is compared to the fragility of life, both human and other. In the end, however, nothing is left, only the originating source, as the narrator's final fragments of the novel dwell on the immortality of the sea: "Solamente el mar no ha dejado de ser" (81; "Only the sea has not ceased to be;" 93). This likelihood of failure, of nothing, is a fact of life. The final pages use images of cancer, mortal fever, a smell of illness, Freud's senselessness, social revolutions, traveling 70 kilometers an hour on a street where donkeys pull carts—or a combination of insanities that render a world truly alienated and replete with despair. In a nutshell, that was reality in the new technological era—one that artists needed to represent in their narrative, as well as having narrative represent its new reality.

Adán goes full circle to reach this conclusion. The opening words, "Ya ha principiado el invierno en Barranco;" "Winter in Barranco has already begun," are followed by a description of winter, the feelings of a child reluctantly plodding off to school, and a commentary on the weather. The second fragment is about the sun and cliffs at the Pacific Ocean's edge; the artist is considering his identity in his surroundings. The cliffs seem to hold the four cardinal points of the world and the likeness of faces of old men in the escarpment:

> Los huesos crujen a compás en el acompasado accionar, en el rítmico tender de las manos al cielo del horizonte . . . .Los mostachos de los viejos cortan finamente, en lonjas como mermelada cara, una brisa

marina y la impregnan de olor de guamanripa, de tabaco tumbesino, de pañuelo de yerbas, de jarabes criollos para la tos (17). The bones creak in time with the timed gestures, with the rhythmic stretching of hands to the sky along the horizon . . . . The old men's whiskers slice into fine strips like expensive jelly the sea breeze and infuse it with the scent of guava trees, tobacco from Tumbes, herb-scented handkerchiefs, Peruvian cough syrups (4).

The smells of marine commerce combine with nature's rocky cliffs, sea, and sky. Then, abruptly, the narrator mentions the "Consulado General de Tomesia, país que hizo Giraudoux . . ." (17; "Consulate General of Tomesia, a country created by Giraudoux;" 4), making note of the well-known French writer Jean Giraudoux, considered an influence on Hispanic avant-garde writers by Susan Nagel (76). By mentioning his name here, Adán raises a flag to warn his readers that his novel would be different. Nagel sees Giraudoux's intentions as similar to a Spanish model:

> Like Cervantes, Giraudoux also sought to deconstruct a genre and often shares his use of literary convention with the reader . . . Thus, his novels are not merely concerned with formal narrative technique but reveal philosophical attitudes as well. Giraudoux's radical techniques of pneumatic metaphor and decharacterization have often been misjudged by critics who have accused him of being a frivolous writer concerned solely with style. They have completely misinterpreted his aims (Nagel 19).

Nagel then quotes from Patricia Waugh to exonerate Giraudoux's metafictional novel and explain its dual role:

> "Metafiction pursues such questions through its formal self-exploration, drawing on the traditional metaphor of the world as a book, but often recasting it in terms of contemporary philosophical, linguistic or literary theory." Waugh believes that the difference between the modern novel and the postmodern novel is that, while the modern novel is concerned with psychology, the postmodern novel is concerned with fictionality and becomes a "metafictional novel" exploding illusion. [Quoting again from Waugh:] "In providing a critique of their own methods of construction, such writings not only examine the fundamental structures of narrative fiction, they also explore the possible fictionality of the world outside the literary fictional test" (19-20).

Giraudoux accepted the universe as a joyful and bountiful experience in contrast to some avant-gardists' solemn assessment of desolate experience. Adán, whether or not influenced by Giraudoux's earliest production (whose first novels appeared in 1909-1910, and principal novels were published in the 1920s), shares his idea that fiction is like life and requires new experience. Adán's metafiction demonstrates that the pursuits of life and the creation of the novel are similar acts affected by political, philosophical, scientific, and linguistic movements. Peruvian critic Luis Alberto Sánchez called Adán "both very young and very old at the same time," for his extreme awareness in his youth when he created this novel (Aguilar Mora 11). He was much ahead of his time in an evironment where traditional realist fiction would continue to predominate until well into the middle of the twentieth century. *La casa de cartón* predates by more than twenty years the renovation in creative fiction undertaken in the 1950s (Higgins 295). Adán had two goals: to renovate Latin American fiction and, much like Giraudoux, examine the intention of constructing a novel.

The plot of Adán's novel is no more than an ephemereal shell for his discourse. The characters, not fully developed, are essentially deconstructed as non-stereotypical characters that merge into the sights, smells, and plants of Barranco. Adán teases the reader with possible information that is never provided; instead, he takes particular memories and develops them into a discourse. He does not overtly tell the reader about the construction of the novel like Palacio does in *Débora*, but the narrator/author pretends to be describing life and Barranco while he develops his artistic theories.

The narrator talks about an ice cream vendor's cart (the vendor's trumpet will open the last fragment of the novel) pulled by an old nag—creating a confluence of new and old technologies. The vendor is representative of the Peruvian:

> El sonar de las ruedas de la carreta en las piedras del pavimento alegra a la fuente las aguas tristes de la pila. El cholo, con mejillas de tierra mojada de sangre y la nariz orvallada de sudor en gotas atómicas, redondas—el cholo carretero no deja pasar la carreta por el césped del jardín ralísimo (18).
>
> The rumble of the cart's wheels on the paving stones gladdens the sad waters of the fountain. The mestizo—his cheeks the color of blood-soaked earth and his nose sprinkled with tiny, round drops of sweat—the mestizo carter does not allow the cart to roll over the lawn of that meager garden (5).

In crisp, scintillating adjectives and descriptions, Adán captures a moment in the hard life of a worker in this vacation town. Reference is made to the toils of the mestizo (mixed indigenous and European race, identified by the pejorative term "cholo" in Peru) often in this novel. In fact, Adán lays the groundwork for writing about racial concerns more than a decade ahead of Peruvian writers Ciro Alegría (1909-1967) and José María Arguedas (1911-1969), who received fame for vividly portraying the conflict between indigenous and European cultures. Adán also makes note of concerns about African race: in the fourth fragment, the narrator begins addressing a "you" which is the narrator's boyhood friend Ramón, who is said to look "mas zambo que nunca" (20; "more Negroid than ever;" 10).

As the narrator reminisces about Ramón, he remembers their discussions of Schopenhauer and Nietzsche; of whom Ramón has read the former and has heard of Neitzsche's "Superman" theories. Adán uses nineteenth century philosophers to show Ramón's backwardness, and suggests that only by rebelling and following irrational impulses—becoming a "nomadic intellectual" outside literary conventions—can the writer create new fiction. There is also an allusion to Spengler, who according to a recent study of *La casa de cartón*, was chosen for his theories stating that intellectuals are a product or cause of their city (Elmore 78).

Ramón was just beginning to live; he was only sixteen years old when they began to discuss philosophies. In the same fragment the narrator says Ramón "era un fracasado" (21; "was a failure;" 11) because he never got the chance to live and explore life. Failure, and also art, is intangible. Ramón, the alter-ego of the narrator, is Everyman: "Y nadie hay que no seas tú o yo" (20; "And there is nobody who is not you or I;" 9). Adán alludes to Determinism, suggesting that no Peruvian—in other words, Everyman—has a way out. Man must follow the path he is destined to follow, which is uncertain, like Ramón's death: "Por esta calle se va al mar, a un mar que nadie ve" (19; "This street leads to the sea, a sea no one sees;" 8). But it is not a traditional determinism, it has an evolutionary route: The sea is where Charles Darwin's theory of evolution says human life began. Our path leads to the sea; we must return. Everyman's life is permeated by the inevitability of these origins. Barranco is "sumergida en agua" and there are even "campanadas mojadas" (18; "sunken under water, and soggy ringing of bells;" 6). That constantly wet ambience will continue forever, but "Ramón en cambio, no volverá nunca" (52; "Ramón, on the other hand, will never return;" 57); the old is gone forever. The narrator places Barranco near the edge of the origins of life, so close to returning to the water that it is always soggy and wet. The artist is also on the edge, attempting to create a new artistic expression with only the subconscious; the tangible is untrustworthy. The narrator is lonely because he is on that edge, alone in his risk and attempt to move toward a new creative expression.

Mario Vargas Llosa (who is greatly responsible for a resurgence in the critical analysis of *La casa de cartón*, due to two essays he published in 1965), considered Adán's novel a better representation of Peruvian reality than the highly acclaimed *El mundo es ancho y ajeno* (1941; *Broad and Alien is the World,* 1945), by Ciro Alegría. Vargas Llosa noted that Adán sacrificed a clarity in plot and structure in order to reach into his inner depths and show the ambience, character, color, and anguish of Barranco (Kinsella 33). In conveying the narrator's loneliness and Barranco's monotony, Adán demonstrates some of the concrete emotions and conflicts of daily suburban life, much as Arqueles Vela did in *El café de nadie.* Adán's novel also prefigures the works of several Peruvian writers of ensuing generations, namely, Vargas Llosa, Julio Ramón Ribeyro (1929-94), and Alfredo Bryce Echenique (1939-).

Specific aspects of the city and plant life help paint Barranco's reality, a modern seaside retreat: streetcars, telephone poles, carts led by donkeys alongside motorcars on the streets, a view of the city from a rooftop, jacaranda plants and fig trees, the bathing resort, the promenades, the breakwaters and the coastal *garúa* (misty rain). In opposition, Lima is captured with references to sticky asphalt streets, filthy movie theaters, and belching oil factories. But Lima also represents the modernity that is reaching Barranco.

The resort suburb and the city are contrasts, and so are many other images. The characters become images that often confuse and merge with others. For example, the narrator associates an English lady, Miss Annie Doll (also called the *gringa* photographer), with the jacaranda plant, and humorously acknowledges his inability to distinguish between the woman and the plant:

Y el jacaranda que está en esa calle es el que yo digo que es la gringa, no sé si es un jacarandá que es la gringa o si la gringa que es un jacarandá. Es el árbol no sé si muy jóven o muy viejo. Ante él dudamos como ante los huacos del Museo, que no sabemos si son de Nazca o de Chimú, si auténticos o falsificados, si negros o blancos. Quizá el jacarandá de la calle Mott es es jóven o viejo a la vez, como la gringa—larguirucho, casi calato del todo . . . que parece haberlo echado el aire (24-25).

And the jacaranda on that street is the one I say is the gringa, or I don't know if it is a jacaranda that is the gringa, or if it is the gringa that is the jacaranda. Whether the tree is very young or very old I don't know. Facing it we have the same doubts as when we face the pieces of pottery in the museums, not knowing if they are from Nasca or Chimu, authentic or falsified, black or white. Perhaps the jacaranda on Mott

Street is both young and old at the same time, like the gringa—lanky, almost completely naked—. . . as if blown there by the wind (17-18).

The jaracaranda "is both young and old at the same time" is a phrase Luis Alberto Sánchez appropriated to describe Adán's work. But the narrator, by using the example of a tree specific to the region, wanted to stress Peru's own history and language.

Other identities are also blurred, creating images in the narrator's memory which are "temblante, oscuro, como en pantalla de cinema," and "a merced de la fuerza que la mueve" (23; "tremulous, dark, as if on a movie screen, and at the mercy of the force that moves it;" 15). This force—muse or subconscious impulse—controls what the narrator reveals. The narrator only describes what he is capable of comprehending, leaving the reader to deduce other information (Lauer 1983, 27).

The narrator/artist begins a commentary on his romantic experiences, called "loves," which bear allusion to muses. He remembers being fourteen years old when his first love was twelve; when things became sexual, she called him a socialist (Silver 21). His second love, who was fifteen, petulant, and ignorant (22), abandoned him like in a tango. His third love was flirtatious and wayward, his fourth was Catita, and his fifth love, who was a "dirty" girl, was the first mortal sin of this seminary student (23). Adán's muse is convoluted. His accounts of a series of loves in his youth stimulate his art. His addresses to Catita display a lively sense of humor and a love for verbal games rather than a serious admission of love. Later in the text, his frustrations with unrequited love indicate his frustration toward artistic production.

The narrator flips through Ramón's diary, remembering childhood friends, Miguel and Manuel, and events that occur along the coast, which read like information from a newspaper: descriptions of a sailing boat race, merchants with exotic foods, a buxom lady, a policeman, Portuguese sailors, heirs to textile mills, and devout women who go to Barranco for health reasons (27). These people, who may have existed in years past, conjure images that may or may not be true.

The diary and/or memory seems to have more intimate details about events at the boarding house run by Ramón's aunt: a 28-year-old public school teacher named Señorita Muller arrives; she dreams of Napoleon on a horse, says "Bon dieu," and only cries when she has a handkerchief (29). One night Ramón penetrates her dreams, the narrator says. She falls in love with him, but Ramón, age 18, does not fall in love with her:

Y un triángulo de palomas vulgares se llevaba los palotes de la Señorita
Muller en el pico, románticamente (35).
And a triangle of vulgar pigeons carried off Señorita Muller's pen
strokes in their beaks, romantically (30).

These specific aspects parody a reality that does not exist; they can
only be images created by memories. Realism is no longer cutting-
edge. The boarding house with its guests and adventures represents
experiences of life which with time become images. The series of early
loves represents a muse or inspiration that will direct realities into
images for the new age.
    Adán parodies Realism and Naturalism. The next fragment
presents another tourist at the boarding house: "un alemán zapatonudo
que olía a cuero y jabón sanitario" (35; "a German wearing thick-soled
shoes and smelling of leather and disinfectant;" 31). His room is full of
spider webs, but it is the preferred room in the house:

Había otro, recién empapelado, y también en alquiler, pero el
telarañoso tenía una gran ventana que daba a un jardín ajeno, lleno de
saucos, con un Eros de yeso y una lora terrible sobre la cabeza de éste
(35).
There was another one, freshly wallpapered and also to let, but the one
with spider webs had a large window facing the neighbor's garden, with
a view of elderberry trees and a plaster of Paris Eros with a terrible
parrot perched on its head (31).

    The German, "gordo y mojado como la mañana" (36; "fat and wet
like the morning;" 32) arrives as Ramón observes him removing his
things from a cart pulled by a mule who has a human name: "La
Martinita, mula inmensa, vieja y mañosa como una tía política" (36;
"Martinita, an enormous, old mule, fussy like an in-law;" 32). Adán
gives objects and animal or plant life nearly human characteristics and
depersonifies human qualities similar to Vela in *El café de nadie*. If
objects and humans have interchangeable qualities, the reader must re-
examine each for an insight not provided by Realism and the
conventional novel:

El pregón de una lechera cayó, inesperado, en medio del cuarto y . . .
las seis campanadas de las seis de la mañana. Las seis campanadas se
las metió Herr Oswald Teller en un bolsillo de la cazadora, y el pregón
de una lechera lo prendió en el peine con que se peinaba la calva . . .
(37).
The cry of the milkmaid fell unexpectedly into the middle of the room,
and . . . so did the church bells ringing six times at six o'clock in the
morning. Herr Oswald Teller stuffed the six bells of six in the morning

into the pocket of his hunting jacket, and the cry of the milkmaid grabbed him by the brush with which he brushed his bald spot . . . (32-33).

Sounds reminiscent of former experiences come into the German's (representing new philosophies and theories) presence, and must be absorbed. When Ramón reaches twenty years old, he listens to music played by the German in his room:

Mozart, liquidado, descendía las escalera y se empozaba en las oquedades como una lluviaza que hubiera traspasado los techos.. . . And Ramón se alargaba en su butaquita, y se endurecía, y escuchaba y acababa mareándose, con una flauta mágica en los tímpanos (37).
Liquified Mozart descended the staircase and formed puddles in the hollows like a torrent of rain that had soaked through the roof.. . . And Ramón drifted away in his armchair and hardened, and listened, and in the end grew dizzy with a magic flute in his eardrums (33).

There is no attempt to describe a reality behind the lives of the residents or visitors, or any sense of encounter with the people themselves. The visitors seem only to represent new ideas and philosophies. The narrator prefers to portray his own subjective perspective, his own map of feeling (Kinsella 35).

Malecón lleno de perros lobos y niñeras inglesas, mar doméstico, historia de familia, el bisabuelo capitán de fragata o filibustero del mar de las Antillas, millonario y barbudo. Malecón con jardines antiguos de rosales débiles y palmeras enanas y sucias; un fox-terrier ladra al sol . . . (39).
The promenade is full of wolfdogs and English nursemaids, a domestic sea, family histories, the great-grandfather who was captain of a frigate, or a freebooter in the sea of Antilles, a bearded millionaire. A promenade of ancient gardens of fragile roses and dirty and dwarfed palm trees; a fox terrier barks at the sun . . . (37).

While John Kinsella defines these feelings as expressions for the sake of feeling or for their subjective quality, Adán (like the other novelists in this study) uses the expression of feelings to represent his search for inspiration, and the people themselves become sketches for characters and thoughts. Old memories, observations, and the imaginative quality that accompanies them are tools of the artist in creating narrative. While Ramón seems to be of inspiration to the artist/narrator, he is more a mentor than a muse.

About halfway through the novel, one fragment concerns a woman who loved him but he did not love in return; she tried to convince him and to forgive him but "yo no lo permití" (42; "I would not allow it;" 41). Rather than document failures in love, Adán wanted to show the frustrations toward artistic production. As an artist, he could not permit any convincing. The Latin American Modernistas expressed their ultimate artistic achievement with a union between mind and body, expressed by the *petit mort*, or climax in the act of lovemaking. Vanguardistas needed to go beyond this Modernista metaphor, and show the frustrations that ensued in reaching for that goal, and the elusive quality of inspiration:

> La cogí de una mano que se escurría como un pez; la arrastré en una dolorosa carrera sobre guijarrones esféricos, hasta la luz y lo desierto; se me ensensibilizaron los talones; tropezamos las manos enlazadas con un riel erecto, inútil, que equilibraba una piedra tonta en la punta, y nos desunimos . . . (41-42).
>
> I grabbed her hand that was as slippery as a fish; I dragged her along toward the light and the desert in a painful race over round pebbles; my heels grew numb; our entwined hands ran into a useless, upright rail that balanced a foolish rock on its end; and we separated . . . (41).

This description of an unhappy relationship aptly portrays the quest for inspiration (as in seeking love), which, when forced, often falls apart. The narrator observes how nature has a will of its own and refuses to stand still; art is similarly stubborn:

> Me alejo del cielo. Y, al salir del campo, limitado por urbanizaciones, advierto que el campo está en el cielo: un rebaño de nubes gordas, vellonosísimas, con premios de Exposición, trisca en un cielo verde. Y esto lo veo de lejos, que me meto en cama a sudar colores (42-43).
>
> I walk away from the sky. And, as I leave the countryside, surrounded by urbanizations, I notice that the countryside is in the sky: a flock of fat, fleecy clouds—award winners at the Exposition—romp about in the green sky. And this I see from far away, so far away that I get into bed to sweat colors (43).

The narrator matures; now he is Catita's lover, and describes the breeze they feel and their view of the street in front of their bedroom window in the early morning. He makes class and racial comments as he watches "una chola bonita, con la cabellera dura, tersa, mojada—talla de barro" (49; a pretty Indian woman, with her hard, shiny, damp head of hair—a mud carving; 52) walk by, whom he is certain must be a kitchen maid. This observation is placed for the reader's abrupt awareness of Peruvian society; they are images to encourage thinking.

The narrator discusses literature as he remembers who he and his friends read while growing up: "Así, nosotros supimos la vida de ese pobre Stephen Dédalus, un cuatro-ojos muy interesante y que mojaba la cama" (49; "this is how we learned about the life of that poor Stephen Dedalus, an interesting man who wore glasses and wet his bed;" 53). James Joyce's character in *Portrait of the Artist as a Young Man* (1915), Stephen Dedalus, is only one of the fictional characters who influence the narrator and his friends and, essentially, the artist. One critic calls Adán a Joycean, Stephen Dedalus-type (Aguilar Mora 10). Adán most likely read the Joyce novel in translation as a teenager or early in the 1920s when he began writing poetry. His narrator in *La casa de cartón* also cites Luigi Pirandello's play, *Six Characters in Search of an Author* (1920), which Adán must have read in the same period of time, and was a strong influence on him:

Así, supimos la trastada que seis personajes jugaron a un buen director de teatro, de cómo le tentaron a escribir y de cómo acabaron no existiendo (49).

In this way we found out about the trick played on a good theater director by six characters, how they enticed him to write and then ended up not existing (53).

The narrator uses this fragment to suggest a new process for narrative fiction, which cannot follow the path (as some contemporary fiction was doing) of traditional narrative, for example, that of the great nineteenth century Spanish novelist: "Y la de Pérez Galdós, práctica y peligrosa, con tísicos y locos y criminales y apestados, pero que el lector ve de lejos sin peligro" (51; "And Pérez Galdós' practical and perilous literature with consumptives and the insane and criminals and the diseased, all of whom the reader sees from afar at no risk to himself;" 55). Adán knows new fiction needs risk. He calls his European contemporaries Pirandello, Joyce, and George Bernard Shaw "idiots" (as he knows he will be called by critics), precisely for taking this risk. Then he makes a pronouncement on how he and his peers were educated:

Nosotros, menos Raúl, nos ateníamos a la olla podrida literaria española y americana. Porque, como en la Insula Barataria, es manjar de canónigos y ricachones (50).

All of us, except Raúl, were steeped in the Spanish and American moldy literary stew. For, like on Sancho's Island of Barataria, it is the food of canon and rich men (54).

Making mention of Don Quijote's sidekick in Cervantes' famous novel, Adán slyly notes that the majority will simply follow tradition in order to be part of the canon, just as Sancho went along with Don Quijote's attempt to be part of an elite tradition. He continues to criticize members of the Spanish canon, subtly demonstrating the influences on his artistic spirit, and others he chooses to discard.

Progressively, each fragment becomes more somber. The next begins with a reference to the end of summer vacation: "Ahora sí que se acabó de veras el verano" (53; "Now the summer is really over;" 58). The narrator and his friend Lucho have gone to the promenade, which they have baptized Proust Boulevard so that it may be ancient, brave, and stand against the "sicológica inmensidad del mar" (52; "psychological inmensity of the sea;" 59). In winter, however, the waves are no longer the sea alongside a street from a French novel, but "un poco de ensoñación para tía solterona" (53; "little bits of daydreams for a spinster aunt;" 59). He and Lucho will return at night and notice the firmament as a cup of coffee with the moon floating as an indissoluble lump of sugar inside; they will conclude:

> Nosotros, previviremos una super vida, quizás verdaderamente futura donde todos los hombres serán hermanos y abstemios, y vegetarianos, y teósofos, y deportistas.. . . ¿qué será? Es posible que no sea nada. O quizá sea ella un verso de Neruda. O quizá una costa de signo . . . . (53).
> We shall prelive a superlife, perhaps actually future in which all men will be brothers and abstemious and vegetarians and theosophists and athletes.. . . What will it be? It might not be anything. Or perhaps it is a verse of Neruda. Or perhaps a symbolic coast . . . . (59).

Adán and his peers must look for new creation, even if it might not be anything. Still, there is the "perhaps." The narrator remembers youthful, post-war dreams with melancholy, then anticipates a future of hopelessness:

> Ser felices un día, ya lo hemos sido tres meses cabales. Y ahora, ¿qué hacemos? ¿Morir? . . . Cuenta, Lucho, cuentos de Quevedo, cópulas brutas, maridos súbitos, monjas sorprendidas, inglesas castas. Dí lo que se te ocurra, juguemos al sicoanálisis, persigamos viejas, hagamos chistes. Todo, menos morir (54).
> To be happy for one day, we have already been happy for three whole months. And now, what should we do? Die?. . . Come on, Lucho, tell tales of Quevedo, brutal copulations, hasty weddings, shocked nuns, chaste Englishwomen. Say whatever comes to mind, let's play at psychoanalysis, follow old ladies, tell jokes. Everything, anything but die (60).

Even if for a short spell (three whole months) the Vanguardia artist can be happy in this moment of the 1920s. Then, he can resume a review of the past in order to create anew. This narrator makes fun of a canonical literary figure and the plots of Spanish sixteenth century novels, but suggests popular culture saves them from death or the end of consciousness. Playing at creating canonical stories is an escape from reaching for the subconscious of creativity.

The next fragment consists of Ramón's "Underwood Poems," which are a collection of strange sayings that read like sketches of words for a rebellious artistic project: "No hay más alegría que la de ser un hombre bien vestido" (55; There is no greater happiness than that of being a well-dressed man), "La ciudad lame la noche como una gata famélica" (55; The city licks the night like a famished cat), and, "La polis griega sospecho que fue un lupanar al que había que ir con revolver" (56; I suspect the Greek city-state was a brothel to be approached with a revolver). These statements, pronouncements on cultural tradition, city life, and the act of living, end with the following: "Estoy sin pasado, con un futuro excesivo. A casa" (59; I have no past, and an excess of future. Let's go home). This strong statement alludes to Peru's own past and future, especially in a literary sense. Peru needs to return to its own roots in order contain an excess of future.

The narrator leaves this idea hanging as he jumps to a fragment explaining Ramón's degenerated state before his death: he spent his time looking under seats in public places, he was a compulsive smoker, he wasted Sundays, and he seemed only to collect his observations of people and life which he put on the Underwood—all actions of an artist. But in this novel it is words, not actions, that are important. Ramón, the narrator's mentor, puts his observations into words. The narrator says he was born with "la boca alegre. Mi vida es una boca que habla, que come, y que sonríe" (68; "a happy mouth; my life is a mouth that speaks, that eats, and that smiles;" 76). Ramón's actions are not as important now as the narrator's words, a suggestion that the present is more important than the past (although the past has influenced him), or tangible reality is more important than memory. That memory is collected from the subconscious to form the words the narrator evokes. Adán shows that consciousness and subconscious join to produce art.

There are no explanations, only suggestions. The narrator simply reminisces: he and Ramón are fifteen years old and watch a woman named Marina wearing only a nightgown as she closes her window each night. Then it is the nighttime promenade again, and the narrator talks about love. The fragment does not disclose who he is talking to, as the narrator pours his heart out:

Tú eres la medida de mi gozo. Tú eres la medida de mi deseo. Detrás de todas las muertes, está el júbilo de reencontrarte en los paraísos terrenales. Amor, cosa pequeña que no crece nunca . . .Eres tonta y linda como todas las mujeres. Tú ríes, y tu risa me reconcilia con la noche.. . . . Ámame, aunque mañana, al despertar, ya no me recuerdes. Ámame, la hora te lo exige. ¡Ay de quien no obedece al tiempo! (63). You are the measure of my pleasure. You are the measure of my desire. Behind all death is the joy of finding you in earthly paradises. Love, a little thing that never grows . . . .You are dumb and pretty like all women. You laugh, and your laughter reconciles me with the night . . .Love me, even if tomorrow, when you awake, you no longer remember me. Love me, the hour demands it of you! Woe to the one who disobeys time! (71)

The narrator could be speaking to Catita or even Ramón, but no clue is given. It is a strong statement of passion and "quizá una obsesa manía de saberlo todo" (66; "perhaps an obsession to know everything;" 75)—a supplication to the artist's muse.

A letter from Catita "huele a soltería—a incienso, a flores secas, a jabón, a yeso, a botica, a leche" (66; "smells of spinsterhood—of incense, dried flowers, soap, plaster, medicine, milk;" 74). These smells are associated with women, and with the male writer's muse, but something is wrong. The traditional muse seems too old, left behind and no longer applicable. The narrator reads some of the letter, and says it states nothing except that she would like to see him with a sad face. That is the desire of the muse of the romantic novel, which was full of sadness and impossible loves: "tu estrella, tan amarga; tu estrella, solterona que se enamora de los cometas imposibles; tu estrella, que te lleva por malos caminos de amor" (67; your star, so bitter; your star: a spinster who falls in love with impossible comets; your star: that leads you down the wrong path of love;" 76).

The traditional muse is bearing down on the artist; he seeks inspiration for his creation, but the old does not fit. He needs a new muse, for a different creation, one that fits the new age. The narrator escapes to the sea—the origin of life—to find a new muse and develop a new art:

¿Ves, Catita? Tú no ves nada porque no estás conmigo en el malecón; pero yo te juro que es así. A mí, en la tarde, frente al mar, el alma se me pone buena, chica, tonta, humana, y se me alegra con los botes pescadores que despliegan la broma de sus velas, y con la candela del cigarrillo—chiquillín colorado que pierde la cabeza en una juguetería azul. Y las altas gaviotas—moscas negras en el tazón aguada del

cielo—me dan ganas de espantarlas con con las manos.. . . . Así es mi
vida, Catita, un charquito en una playa (67, 69).
You see, Catita? You don't see anything because you are not with me
on the promenade above the sea; but I swear to you it is just as I say. In
the afternoon, facing the sea, my soul becomes good, small, silly,
humane, and is gladdened by the fishing boats that unfurl their joke of a
sail, and by the burning ember of the cigarette—a red-haired child who
loses his head in a blue toy shop. And high-flying bulls—black flies in
the sky's mug of watery milk—make me want to shoo them away with
my hands.. . . . Such is my life, Catita—a little puddle on the beach (75-
76, 78).

The narrator's descriptive qualities, or his imagination unleashed,
are the tools for creation of the new novel. Adán cannot soar through
the sky to create his art; tradition (which thinks in terms of continuing
rivers) does not inspire him:

. . . No creo que nuestra vida tenga relación alguna con las estrellas.
¡Ah Catita! La vida no es un río que corre; es una charca que se
corrompe.. . . . Mi vida es un hoyito cavado en la arena de una playa por
las manos de un niño novillero . . . ya ves tú porque no puede
entristecerme (69).
. . . I do not believe our lives have any relationship whatsoever with the
stars. Oh, Catita! Life is not a river that flows: life is a puddle that
stagnates . . . . My life is a hole dug in the sands of a beach by the
hands of a truant child . . . now you see why I cannot get sad (77-78).

He cannot be a romantic (he is not sad) or a rational writer. Things
are not as they used to be; in this technological society artistic pursuit is
a stagnating puddle, looking for new ways to create. The narrator seeks
new life for his creation; he looks to the sea for new inspiration while
talking to Catita, the old muse. Catita suggests the idea of sexual
vitality and energy that attracts the narrator; the old muse must be
changed. By the end of the novel Catita and the sea become
interchangeable and fuse into a single being that encompasses life and
language: "Catita, mar de amor, amor de mar. Catita, cualquier cosa y
ninguna cosa. Catita, todas las vocales apareciendo en ella, cabal,
íntegra" (74; "Catita, sea of love, love of sea. Catita, anything and
nothing. Catita, appearing in all the vowels, whole, complete;" 85).
The inspiration is now new.
       The constant overlapping of experience throughout the novel, the
similarity of Ramón's diary and the narrator's story, and their shared
feelings toward Catita, lead the reader to assume Adán is trying to
describe a single state of mind (Kinsella 35). Ramón's description is a
subjective one, for it is the narrator's perception of Ramón. He prefers

to recall him as an icon: "Yo sueño con una iconografía de Ramón, que me permitiera recordarle a él, tan plástico, tan espacial, plásticamente, espacialmente" (81; "I dream of an iconography of Ramón that would allow me to remember him, so plastic, so special [sic], plastically, spatially;" 93). Ramón is also representative of Peru, in the sense of Rodo's *Ariel*—a way to find new literature in a new era that is Peru's own.

The implication of this remembrance is that the narrator chooses to recognize another person's reality in terms of a collection of plastic or spatial representations, that is, through images that he projects onto the character. Thus, it is scarcely the other person's reality, but rather the narrator's own highly subjective impressions of what he sees in his mind (Kinsella 36). He expresses the idea further:

> Todos somos imágenes concebidas en un trozo amplio y calmoso, imágenes que se folian, o se enyesan y fenestran, o se visten de dril, o se ciman con casquete de vidrio (87).
> We are all images conceived during a calm and supple trot [sic], images that become foliated, plastered, and fenestrated, or are clothed in drill, or topped with a glass helmet (99).

People symbolically understand life through imagery, but the images are always changing, never restricted to an artist's representation of reality or any fixed rendering. The only possible permanence is that of change, therefore, the process is favored over the product (Elmore 81). Here the process is that of opening the door to art.

On the one hand, *La casa de cartón* is rich in sensuous imagery which strives to convey myriad sensations and emotions underneath the surface reality of Barranco, or, as Vargas Llosa points out, the truest version of reality in Peru (Kinsella 36). On the other hand, the novel is limited by the subjective perceptions of a shy, sensitive youth whose consciousness filters the images. He is a youth who has difficulty communicating with others, preferring to project his own images onto them. The title of the novel is an analogue of literature itself, a "house" of fiction where life and imagination are defined by the flimsy "cardboard" materials of language (Kinsella 36), and shifting subconscious states of mind. If Ramón is the narrator's alter ego, the house is a retreat for artistic imagination, from which the author can gaze uninhibitedly at the Peruvian landscape.

La casa de cartón could be easily interpreted as surrealistic fiction of dreamlike quality where the author/narrator's subconscious speaks. But Adán's poetic prose furthers his discourse with the use of Expressionism (mostly unrecognized in his day). Fresh from Germany after World War I, Expressionism—a movement that began among painters—provided a way for the artist to reach deeper into the subconscious (Schwartz 402). Adán tries to go further than Modernismo, and to an originally Peruvian state. The narrator's disillusion and sentiments are more intensely portrayed by the strong and exaggerated descriptions of smell and sound. The external reality dissolves into the quiet and melancholy consciousness of the village Barranco, which is described from the interior perspective of one of its own inhabitants, the narrator.

The subconscious is represented in three metaphors recurring throughout the novel: "campo" (field), "mar" (sea), and "cielo" (sky). By the end of the novel, all three come together as the narrator nostalgically recalls the previous summer:

> El mar es también las afueras de la ciudad. Ahora el mar es un espejo donde se mira el cielo, un grueso y vasto cristal azogado de lizas y corvinas. El mar está verde porque el cielo está verde. El cielo, rostro inmenso, sin facciones y verde . . . . El cielo puede ser un campo agrícola o pecuario. Pero no; ahora es un rostro que se mira en el espejo del mar (85-86).
> The sea is also the outskirts of the city. Now the sea is a mirror that reflects the sky, a thick and enormous looking glass quicksilvered with mullets and corbinas. The sea is green because the sky is green. The sky, immense face, green and featureless . . . .The sky can be a field for farming or livestock. But it isn't; now it is a face that looks at itself in the mirror of the sea (98).

Adán reverses the accepted idea of reflected color by noting the green of the sea in relation to the green of the sky, instead of the reflection of the blue in the sky turning the sea blue. The sea is furthermore pictured as a face without features, only color. The metaphor of the countryside strikes his imagination, but he returns to the original metaphors of face and mirror. The narrator is recalling the green and pleasant days of summer, and his concentration on physical reality reveals his nostalgia. In fact, Ramón introduced the narrator to the vital pleasures of life during the beautiful summer months (94). With Ramón dead and winter upon him, the past seems gone forever, lingering only, and forever, in the narrator's memory. But what is stronger—conscious or subconscious reality? While a nostalgic past is gone, the modern era can portray both a heritage and a present, if the subconscious is accessed.

Hanging in the balance are life and imagination, both of which seem to fascinate the narrator/author (Unruh 112). While one Barranco street ends at the sea, another ends in an open field on the edge of town.

He imagines those boundaries—the sea and a field—changing in the future as the city expands. They remind him of limits between the human and non-human worlds, and between life and death. According to Vicky Unruh these boundaries are undefined sites of transformations, harbingers of what is yet to unfold—both in life and in fiction. Boundary positions point metaphorically to the artist's desire within the vanguardista spirit to keep a distance from his surroundings while immersing himself in them (113). Blurred dimensions or boundaries are fundamental to the artistic process, and to the artist's ambivalent engagement with a changing world. The artist is not composed of one figure or one dimension—the narrator and/or Ramón his alter-ego—just as the muse, the source of inspiration, blurs distinctions from woman to man to woman. In the penultimate fragment, animal and human life (including technology or science) are blurred:

> La tarde proviene de esta mula pasilarga, tordilla, despaciosa. De ella emanan, en radiaciones que invisibiliza la iluminación de las tres posmeridiano y revela el lino de la atmósfera—pantalla de cinematográfico, pero redonda y sin necesidad de sombra—de ella emanan todas las cosas. Al fin de cada haz de rayos—una casa, un árbol, un farol, yo mismo. Esta mula nos está creando al imaginarnos. En ella me siento yo solidario en origen con lo animado y lo inanimado. Todos somo imágenes concebidas en un trozo amplio y calmoso, imágenes que se folian, o se enyesan y fenestran, o se visten de dril, o se ciman con casquete de vidrio (86-87).
>
> The afternoon arises from this slow-moving, dapple-gray mule with a long stride. From her emanates—in waves that make visible the light of three o'clock postmeridian and reveal the canvas of the atmosphere—the movie screen, a round one that does not need darkness; from her all things emanate. At the end of each bundle of rays: a house, a tree, a lamp, myself. This mule is creating us as it imagines us. Through her I feel the solidarity of my origins with the animate and the inanimate. We are all images conceived during a calm and supple trot, images that become foliated, plastered, and fenestrated, or are clothed in drill, or topped with a glass helmet (99).

Whether life or an artistic creation, we are all "conceived images." These images have no borders, for they are blurred to include the imagined, real, constructed, and always changing.

A conception of boundaries, edges, and ends of roads strongly suggests consciousness, while their blurring suggests subconsciousness. While the argument is well made by critic John Kinsella for subconscious motivation—pursued by Adán's innovative peers in the 1920s—Adán's narrative vacillates between conscious and subconscious inclinations, either to tease the reader or to suggest a new outlook on creation. The narrator's memory is, of course, not his conscious state, but when he attempts to paint images and construct a new reality, it is his conscious state that does so. Mikhail Bakhtin, writing at approximately the same time as Martín Adán, believed the conscious state was the more powerful: "Consciousness is far more frightening than all unconscious complexes." That is because, for Bakhtin, "at the bottom of man" we find not the Id but the other (Todorov 33).Bakhtin was opposed to the idea of psychological inspiration, finding that the artist was always cognizant of his discourse with the "other." Adán, however, effectively shows the process from inspiration (nostalgic memories) to artistic creation, or tangible realizations.

Toward the end of the novel, Adán describes how, after thoughts leave one's head, the conscious state remains observing, stepping, or tripping over an unfortunate human being on the street. These experiences lead to a consciousness of images:

Una paloma se ha llevado mi último buen pensamiento. Ahora soy yo como soy verdaderamente, limpio, asiático, fino, malo. Ahora llevo cuello redondo de caucho. Ahora salto por sobre una pobre vieja cegatona (83).
A dove has carried away my last good thought. Now I am as I truly am: clean, Asiatic, refined, bad. Now I have a round-rubber neck. Now I jump over an old woman who examines her shoe on the street, poor old blind woman (95).

Finally, the narrator speaks to his "you" about wrestling between conscious and subconscious states. Everything in life, in Barranco, represents these opposites:

Tú desapareces a cada instante de mi conciencia, y al volver, estás cálida, como el sombrero o un libro que olvidamos a pleno sol cuando huímos a la sombra. La calle ancha nos abre los ojos, violenta, hasta dolernos y cegarnos. Todo el pueblo se arrastra—postes, árboles, gentes, calles—a las orillas de este arroyo de frescura y brisas del mar. En el horno de verano, humean las casas, de masa de pan, y se requeman por debajo. Ya no vienes tú a mi lado (90).
You disappear from my consciousness every instant, and when you return, you are warm, like the hat or the book we leave in the bright sun when we escape to the shade. The wide street opens our eyes, violently, until it hurts and blinds us. The whole town drags itself along—posts, trees, people, streets—along the banks of this stream of freshness and sea breezes. In the oven of sun, the houses made of

bread dough bake and get burned on the bottom. You no longer walk by my side (103).

Once the narrator feels the heat of the sun and hears the church bells, he finds himself deeply aware of exterior reality. The artist may tap into the subconscious state for his inspiration, but he will never be far from awareness of the reality in which he lives. The possibility seems important enough for Adán to place this reflection near the end of the novel.

In the final fragment of *La casa de cartón*, there is a gentle admonition that the artist can no longer be still, contemplating the "indoors" or inner being of the subconscious (103). The blurred positions of Ramón and the narrator, Ramón and Catita, Catita and the sea, and other characters depict not only the changing world and the artist's necessity to change with it, but also the blurring of influences (muses) and stylistic techniques in the construction of the novel. The artist is a workman, not simply a creator (as previous literary generations thought); as a producer of texts, he must relate to the stimuli around him. He believes in the permanence of change and wants to keep his senses sharp to create along with change, or even ahead of it, if he is to be a nomadic intellectual.

Critics did not recognize Adán's work as incipient new narrative, instead relegating novels such as *La casa de cartón* to fragments of poetic words without structure, or the work of a clever, but inexperienced young person (Lindstrom 71). Perhaps because he created this novel when he was only 20 years old, his work was not taken seriously, but Gabriel García Márquez (1928-) also wrote *One Hundred Years of Solitude* when he was 20 years old, years later understanding the meaning in it (now called Magical Realism) and refining it for publication. Adán's novel *La casa de cartón* also contained the meaning of new, twentieth century narrative fiction, and is only recently being understood as such.

---

[i] The cold offshore waters had for years attracted large numbers of fish, which in turn attracted birds, who left their droppings on islands near the coast. Atmospheric dryness aided the preservation and calcination of these droppings, known as guano, which had a high concentration of nitrogen. As the Incas had known, guano was a superb fertilizer (Skidmore 191).

[ii] All English quotes from Adán's novel in this chapter will be based on her translation.

CHAPTER SIX

CONCLUSION:
THE VANGUARDIA LEGACY

The Vanguardia years, which reached a high point in Latin America in the late 1920s, were a rich period of ferment and radical change due to technological invention, economic growth, political tension, and a proliferation of European-inspired artistic movements. Vanguardia artists not only shared a common impatience with established conventions, but also sought extreme theoretical positions on literature. They searched for superior meaning and a representation of the artistic subconscious, while attempting to represent their respective urban Latin American communities—the new metropolises of the twentieth century. Like their European peers, they created new narrative fiction that defied linear structure, space and time, character development, and traditional plot. They were often called crazy (Arlt and Palacio), and many have been forgotten or overshadowed by later novelists' achievements. Their "madness" may have come from trying to reach a previously unattained state of consciousness that Freud's theories introduced, but which remained elusive to many writers. Arqueles Vela, Roberto Arlt, Pablo Palacio, and Martín Adán understood the frustration and difficulty of creating new narrative and, for that reason, chose to portray the evolution of the creative act in their fiction, as well as create a discourse on the need for new creation.

The question could be asked: What makes a novel a novel? Even in the postmodern era, the question is seldom answered definitively, but there is a broader understanding today of the artist's intentions in creating a novel than in the 1920s. Postmodern theory provides a new opportunity to reread these early novels for greater depth. Today we understand that the novel does not always have a tidy beginning, climax, and end; similarly, life is seldom so neatly explained (Trinh Minh-ha 143). Now it is easier to see the Vanguardia writer's reason for rebelling. In order to be new, and continue to evolve, twentieth century fiction had to reconstruct the boundaries (Haraway 181) of traditional literature by loosening its bindings (Spivak 263).

A comparison could be made between narrative fiction and painting in the Vanguardia era. Spanish painter Salvador Dalí (1904-1989) initiated revolutionary art as a surrealist, influenced by earlier artistic movements and Freud's writings. Surrealism, launched in 1924, sought "pure psychic automatism through which it is intended to express, verbally or in any other way, the true functioning of thought . . . outside any moral or esthetic preoccupation" (Ades 72). Avant-garde writers were also interested in the implications of Freud's discoveries for the liberation of the human imagination, which correlated with a world of rapid technological change. Latin American Vanguardia writers sought to express thought without the constraints of traditional rules of language and structure, as they incorporated a search for the particular identities of their countries. According to Bakhtin, the novel is the sole genre that continues to evolve and develop, it is never completed. He thought the novel would be as important for the twentieth century as the epic was in the ancient world. Donna Haraway has pointed out that we needed to reconstruct boundaries because matter and imagination are in continual interaction. Thus, there are only partial perspectives. And according to Linda Hutcheon, no narrative can be a master narrative.

The novels analyzed in this study demonstrate a break with previous generations and the creation of a new, innovative style that has clearly influenced subsequent twentieth century narrative fiction. The concepts, images, and discourse which linger in our minds after reading these novels are indicative of the novelists' desire for the reader to exercise the Brechtinian concept of thinking rather than identifying. Vela, Arlt, Palacio, and Adán were aware not only of the need for the novel to keep pace with worldwide economic and political change, but also the need for the reader's involvement in its evolutionary creation. They were not introverted, esthetically-concerned artists like their Modernista or Romantic predecessors. They sought to be a part of changing technology and science; in fact, they recognized, as their contemporary Mikhail Bakhtin did, that the rapid technology and intense activity of the new century enhanced the novel's evolution:

> All the already completed genres had been formed during eras of closed and deaf monoglossia. In contrast to other major genres, the novel emerged and matured precisely when intense activization of external and internal polyglossia was at the peak of its activity (12).

By becoming "organically receptive" to new forms of perception, reading, and other outside stimuli, the modern novel could become as important for the contemporary world as the epic had become for the ancient world (10).

In order to produce the new novel, these writers sought to show its formulation—its creation—within its discourse. The muse, apparent madness, lack of characterization, and an abstract sense of time and structure are their tools. The unifying theme of these novels is based on: (1) the portrayal of inspiration and creation of the new novel; and (2) the need for a Latin American identity. The search for artistic creation is enhanced by an awareness of American in combination with European cultural values (Forster 8). While these novels are expressly Latin American, they have specific Mexican, Argentinian, Ecuadorean, and Peruvian attributes.

El café de nadie calls on technological muses while it critiques conventional forms of the novel. Vela's muse is one that moves him through thought processes that bring about new forms of narrative fiction. This author exposes hegemonic ideologies and structures with irony and parody, seeming to "play" while revealing his own efforts at artistic creation. There are several states of consciousness in the novel, each set in an urban environment where the narrator is trying to embrace the muse of technology. Upon creating his fiction, Vela explains the Mexican artist's attempt to supersede previous generations with a representation of twentieth century, urban life. He situates the events of his novel in Mexico City—a café frequented by writers, streetcars, and apartment buildings, all aspects of the new metropolis. It is the city he thinks of when he takes a train to the province, in fact, the train represents the thought process that takes him from and returns him to the city.

Los siete locos is a desperate search for identity. Lacking a muse, the characters are guided by their own paranoias and disparate perspectives, portraying an attempt to escape from conventional form, and the dehumanizing pressures created by increasing urbanization, insecurity, and loneliness. The rapid changes in states of conscience—from cynicism to self-compassion to sado-masochism—reflect a search for true consciousness not only of the individual but also of Argentine identity. Will powers from outside—fascism and the Ku Klux Klan—affect Argentine identity or will its people find their own path, create their own story? The novelistic tension that comes from the superior knowledge of the reader over the character Erdosain, reveals Arlt's criticism of society's invention and manipulation of artistic creation. The final trick is to have the reader connect with Erdosain and acknowledge his own state as neither madman nor savior but as a complex human consciousness. In the end, the character has the final word; his story continues outside the novel. In this way, artistic expression is no longer manipulated but left open to the reader.

In *Débora*, Pablo Palacio's character is the primary instrument of frustration, a character annoyingly undeveloped while the search for Débora goes unfulfilled or becomes an illusion. Here the artist defiantly manipulates the characters (the two lieutenants), abruptly stopping their conversations. While Palacio makes socio-political denunciations of his society, and parodies the popular soap opera or detective story, he accomplishes much more in his discourse. His use of a biblical prophetess' name indicates the influence or guidance of outside forces in inspiration. But he shows that the artistic search will be frustrated if it only considers the foreign. The artist must synthesize the outside influences and create from within; it is an internal agony The ultimate creation should be Ecuadorean, despite Latin American Modernista or European influence. The narrator's final words are to "suppress the minutiae" (Realism, Romanticism) and seek the "outline of a soft, white color"; in other words, to seek new creation rather than imitate. Palacio demonstrates the artist's power to create by engaging the narrator with the character and the reader. If the "minutiae" are put to rest to make space for new fiction, the character and reader will have a role to play; in fact, the Lieutenant dies the death of the conventional novel so that new creation may begin. Pablo Palacio's discourse is an explanation of possibilities and renewal in art.

Finally, the narrator in *La casa de cartón* attempts to connect past realities with the present, in an artistic effort to unite subconscious impulses with conscious ones. Field, sea, and sky metaphors surge from the narrator's subconscious, and play with spatial/temporal boundaries as well as conscious states of reality. Adán's narrator focuses on the boundaries of Barranco, Lima, the human and animal worlds, life and death, and then blurs them to reveal the artist's engagement with a changing world. This blurring of boundaries represents what is yet to unfold artistically. No dimension is perfectly tangible, all are "conceived images." Adán vacillates between consciousness and subconsciousness to show a new outlook on creation. Everything in Barranco, or life, represents these opposing states, demonstrating Adán's idea that although the artist may tap into his subconscious for inspiration, he will never be far from a conscious reality. While Barranco must retain its native identity, it is also being affected by each new foreign, political, and technological arrival. Likewise, the novel of the twentieth century would be both old and new, distorted and enduring.

Adán and Arlt humorously manipulate aspects of modernization with metaphors (Elmore 79). Thereby, advances in society are used to show a need for advances in prose fiction. Vela makes a joke of the detective story, and Palacio of his military lieutenant. Each novelist uses humor to attack the promposity and dogmatism of a previous generation, to bring a healthy skepticism to art. This provides a distancing effect, forcing the reader to think about what is being presented, a strategy that has been called a "pedagogy of laughter," by some critics (Beverley 129).

These novelists are not simply committing anarchy as Gustavo Pérez Firmat affirms in his study on the Vanguardia; rather, they are seeking a new vision, a personal poetics. They do not create art solely for artistic criticism, but to explain its changing nature. Their characters exist for the purpose of debating artistic concerns (Unruh 82-83). With this rebellion of the traditional character, Vanguardia writers set the stage for Latin American Boom literature:

> The character—who represents man within the novel—is the mobilizer; it is he who provokes the linguistic concentration from which a recognizable form is composed. In his turn, if the reader understands this form it is because he shares a way of being with the characters—because both participate in the same system—he identifies with them because through them the signs which reside in the text become decipherable to him. On his side, the author constructs his characters following the effective or virtual pattern which he knows in people, he singularizes them by respecting, varying, and denying certain models, the selection of which surely constitutes the first stage in the genesis of a novel (Jitrik 164).

In their studies, Merlin H. Forster and Vicky Unruh hold that the Vanguardia artists destroy old structures out of rebellion against old science, i.e., logic and reason, and to make way for new science and philosophy. Eminent Latin American writer Ernesto Sábato called structuralism "valid to the point at which it ceases to be so" (150). The Vanguardia writers emphasized abstract qualities and a lack of structure that would later become more noticeable and have an impact on the postmodern novel. For the Vanguardia artists, a disparate structure defined their discourse; but it would also establish a model:

> The twentieth century novel not only provides an account of a more complex and truer reality than that of the previous century, but has also acquired a metaphysical dimension it did not possess before. . . .It is evident, however, that this general crisis of civilization was necessary for it to have acquired its terrible timeliness in the way that when a ship is sinking the passengers abandon their games and frivolities to face the great final problems which were nevertheless latent in their ordinary lives. The novel of today . . . not only has launched itself on the

exploration of territories not even suspected by those novelists but it has taken on philosophic and cognitive dignity (Sábato 100).

While Pérez Firmat identifies a Vanguardia period in the Spanish-speaking world, he sees the pursuit as a "vacation" from the literary canon (33). But Forster, Unruh, and other critics (i.e., María del Carmen Fernández and David William Foster), note the importance of Vanguardia artists as an influence on subsequent generations of writers of Latin American fiction. Other Vanguardia novelists should be explored for their contributions and influences on the contemporary novel, especially with the opportunities provided by contemporary theory and new readings.

It would be interesting, for example, to study specific writers in the extensive Vanguardia movement in the Caribbean and Central American nations. Although artistic activity began a little later, Cuba and Nicaragua were especially prolific (Forster 108). A search for "pure" poetry in Cuba led, for example, to the *sones* and Afro-Caribbean poetry by such figures as Nicolás Guillén (1902-1989). Cuban Vanguardia writers who would make interesting studies are Eugenio Florit (1903-1982), Mariano Brull (1891-1956), and Emilio Ballagas (1908-1954). Merlin Forster's bibliography is an excellent first source to pick up trails and ideas. Nicaragua's Vanguardia literary expression began late in the 1920s and was responsive to unique national and cultural concerns as well as experimentation (Forster 133). Pablo Antonio Cuadra (1912-) is one of the principal figures who needs more critical attention, and others include Joaquín Pasos (1914-1947) and José Coronel Urtecho (1906-1983). Nicaraguan Vanguardia and social realist literature owe some debt to Rubén Darío (1867-1916), for his recognition that Northern forces would weaken and attempt to control the rest of America, affecting cultural production. Although his poetry is mostly aesthetic, he also initiates a radical form of nationalism, and suggests "a path of development different from simple assimilation to U.S. hegemony or oligarchic immobilism." Early twentieth century poets, while apolitical, "projected a cosmic utopian subjectivism that is still an important strain in Nicaraguan political poetry" (Beverley 59). Nicaraguan Vanguardists, then, were nationalist, anti-*yanqui*, and antibourgeois, proposing a need for armed struggle against U.S. intervention, and for placing great value on Nicaragua's indigenous past (61). The Nicaraguan Vanguardia voice was one of the strongest for the need to find the roots of cultural production in the masses, the peasants, and even the indigenous cosmology.

There is an important gap in studies specifically on women writers of Vanguardia. Women writers and intellectuals in the 1920s (and for decades after) had little access to primarily male-dominated vanguardist activities, and its focus on popular culture (Unruh 28). Contributions by women were strong in Peru and Brazil, but few studies on individual women writers exist. Only Francine Masiello and Vicky Unruh have published research on women writers in the Vanguardia.

More work is needed to uncover those ignored contributions to early innovative narrative. Many interesting authors of narrative fiction could be examined for their avant-garde contributions to the modern novel, as well as their drive to incorporate a sense of true Latin American origins. Latin American writers will always write in Spanish, thanks to the conquest, but many writers have felt a need to identify their own origins as well as their struggles against imperialism. The Cuban Revolution was of great impact on some Boom writers and their innovative fiction, just as the first World War and U.S. intervention in parts of Latin America were of influence on Vanguardia writers. Neil Larsen has noted that while early twentieth century Latin American fiction betrays "superficial traits of outside influence, [it] transforms the foreign element into a radically original compound" (50). As with Brazilian anthropomorphy, Latin American writers show that even though they ingest European influence, as it goes into their system, what comes out is more Latin American than European. In essence, literature throughout the twentieth century demonstrates a continuation of radical break from past centuries and a need to express true Latin Americaness. Even so, as Larsen points out:

> The literature that lays the tacitly least controversial claim to modernity
> is that of the so-called *generación del boom*, a group of writers of
> narrative fiction mainly, of whom several are still active and in whose
> shadow much contemporary Latin American writing continues to be
> produced" (50).

It is the early twentieth century, revolutionary narrative that can be especially revealing for the launching of a true Latin American voice.

While this study has highlighted only four innovative authors of Vanguardia narrative fiction from four different countries, many more studies remain to be done. Many writers for five decades before the Boom contributed to the creation of *new* Latin American narrative; their works offer interesting research. More publications in English will help correlate the achievements of Anglo-Saxon Modernism in the early twentieth century with the Latin American Vanguardia.

The Vanguardia era was not only a celebration of technology, it was also a plea to see the need for modernization in fiction, and in Latin America, for the need to reveal its own identity. There was an exciting belief in the 1920s that the old régimes of politics and culture were over, but at the same time, a fear of new controls that would impede human progress. *El café de nadie, Los siete locos, Débora*, and *La casa de cartón* are expressions of those feelings in the exciting and tumultuous era of Vanguardia, and, with their discourse and recreation of the components of narrative fiction, the forerunners of the twentieth century novel.

BIBLIOGRAPHY

Adán, Martín. *La casa de cartón*. Lima: Editorial Juan Mejía Baca, 1971.

Ades, Dawn. *Salvador Dalí*. London: Thames and Hudson Ltd., 1982.

Agosín, Marjorie. "María Luisa Bombal: Biography of a Story-telling Woman." *Knives and Angels: Women Writers in Latin America*. Ed. Susan Bassnett. London: Zed Books Ltd. (1990): 26-35.

Aguilar Mora, Jorge. *Martín Adán: El más hermoso crepúsculo del mundo*. México: Fondo de Cultura Económica, 1992.

Alegría, Fernando. "Antiliterature." *Latin America in its Literature*. New York: Holmes and Meier Publishers (1980): 181-199.

Anderson Imbert, Enrique. *Historia de la literatura hispanoamericana II*. México: Fondo de Cultura Económica, 1966.

Arlt, Roberto. *Los siete locos*. Buenos Aires: Editorial Losada, 1985 (6th ed.).

Bakhtin, M.M. *The Dialogic Imagination: Four Essays*. Trans. Caryll Emerson and Michael Holquist. Ed. Michael Holquist. Austin: U of Texas P, 1981.

Barrett, William. "Writers and Madness." *Literature and Psychoanalysis*. Ed. Edith Kurzweil and William Phillips. New York: Columbia UP (1983): 85-100.

Begley, Adam. "Harold Bloom: Colossus among Critics." *The New York Times Magazine* (Sep. 25, 1994): 32-35.

Beja, Morris. *James Joyce: A Literary Life*. Columbus: Ohio State UP, 1992.

Beverley, John and Marc Zimmerman. *Literature and Politics in the Central American Revolutions*. Austin: U of Texas P, 1990.

Bialostosky, Don. "Dialogic Criticism." *Contemporary Literary Theory*. Ed. G. Douglas Atkins and Laura Morrow. Amherst: U of Massachusetts P (1989): 214-228.

Bradbury, Malcolm. "A Geography of Modernism: London 1890-1920." *Modernism: A Guide to European Literature*. London: Penguin (1976): 172-190.

Brushwood, John. *Mexico in its Novel*. Austin: U of Texas P, 1966.

Bullock, Alan. "The Cultural and Intellectual Climate of Modernism: The Double Image." *Modernism: A Guide to European Literature 1890-1930.* Ed. Malcolm Bradbury and James Walter McFarlane. London: Penguin (1976): 57-70.Bürger, Peter. *Theory of the Avant-Garde.* Trans. Michael Shaw. Minneapolis: U of Minnesota P, 1984.

Burgos, Fernando. "La vanguardia hispanoamericana y la transformación narrativa (en Ecuador y Chile)." *Nuevo Texto Crítico* 2.3 (1989): 57-169.

Bustos Fernández, María. *Vanguardia y renovación en la narrativa latinoamericana.* Madrid: Editorial Pliegos, 1996.

Carrión, Benjamín. "La literatura más atrevida que se ha hecho en el Ecuador." *Recopilación de textos sobre Pablo Palacio.* Ed. Reinaldo Castilla. Habana: Casa de las Américas (1987): 29-46.

Cohan, Steven and Linda M. Shires. *Telling Stories: A Theoretical Analysis of Narrative Fiction.* New York: Routledge, 1988.

Corral, Wilfrido H. "Colindantes sociales y literarios en los fragmentos de la novela *Débora.*" *Recopilación de textos sobre Pablo Palacio.* Habana: Casa de las Américas (1987): 349-369.

Cortázar, Julio. "Literatura en la revolución y revolución en la literatura: Algunos malentendidos a liquidar." *Literatura en la revolución y revolución en la literatura.* México: Siglo Veintiuno Editores (1970): 38-77.

Cosse, Rómulo. "El café de nadie y las vanguardias hispanoamericanas." *Estridentismo: memoria y valoración.* Ed. Esther Hernández Palacios. México: Fondo de Cultura Económica (1983): 176-188.

Cuesta, Jorge. "¿Existe una crisis en nuestra literatura de vanguardia?" *Las Vanguardias literarias en hispanoamérica.* Ed. Hugo J. Verani. México: Fondo de Cultura Económica (1990): 105-107.

Dahl, Mari. "Reacciones frente al espejo palaciano: La condena, la locura y la modernidad." *Dactylus* 12 (1993): 71-83.

D'haen, Theo. "Postmodern Fiction: Form and Function." *Neophilologus* 71.1 Jan. 1987: 144-153.

Donoso, José. *Historia personal del "boom".* Barcelona: Seix Barral, 1983.

Elmore, Peter. *Los muros invisibles: Lima y la modernidad en la novela del siglo XX.* Lima: Mosca Azul, 1993.

Fernández, María del Carmen. *El realismo abierto de Pablo Palacio: En la encrucijada de los 30.* Quito: Ediciones Libri Mundi, 1991.

Fernández Retamar, Roberto. "Intercommunication and New Literature." *Latin America in its Literature*. Ed. César Fernández Moreno. New York: Holmes & Meier Publishers (1972): 245-259.

Flores Jaramillo, Renán. *Los huracanes: Pablo Palacio, Jorge Icaza, Oswaldo Guayasamin*. Madrid: Editora Nacional, 1979.Forster, Merlin H. and K. David Jackson. *Vanguardism in Latin American Literature: An Annotated Bibliographical Guide*. New York: Greenwood Press, 1990.

Foster, David William. *Currents in the Contemporary Argentine Novel*. Columbia: U of Missouri P, 1975.

Franco, Jean. *Plotting Women: Gender and Representation in Mexico*. New York: Columbia UP, 1989.

----, *An Introduction to Spanish-American Literature*. New York: Cambridge UP, 1969.

----, *The Modern Culture of Latin America*. New York: Frederick A. Praeger Publishers, 1967.

Fuentes, Carlos. *La nueva novela hispanoamericana*. México: Joaquín Mortiz, 1980 (original ed. 1969).

Gnutzmann, Rita. "Redescubrimiento de un pionero." *Letras de Deusto* 16.36 (Sept-Dec. 1986): 153-159.

González, Otto-Raúl. "Conocimiento y reconocimiento del estridentismo." *Estridentismo: memoria y valoración*. Ed. Esther Hernández Palacios. México: Fondo de Cultura Económica (1983): 80-94.

Gordon, Samuel. "Modernidad y Vanguardia en la Literatura Mexicana: Estridentistas y Contemporáneos." *Revista Iberoamericana* 55.148-149 (July-Dec. 1989): 1083-1098.

Haraway, Donna. *Simians, Cyborgs, and Women: The Reinvention of Nature*. New York: Routledge, 1991.

Hart, Stephen. "Current Trends in Scholarship on *Modernismo*." *Neophilologus* 71.2 (April 1987): 227-233.

Higgins, James. "Two Poet-Novelists of Peru." *Hispanic Studies in Honour of Geoffrey Ribbans*. Liverpool: Liverpool UP (1992): 289-296.

Hitchcock, Peter. *Dialogics of the Oppressed*. Minneapolis: U of Minnesota P, 1993.

Hutcheon, Linda. *Irony's Edge: The Theory and Politics of Irony*. New York: Routledge, 1994.

----, "Beginning to Theorize Postmodernism." *A Postmodern Reader*. Albany: State U of New York P (1993): 243-272.

----, *A Poetics of Postmodernism: History, Theory, Fiction*. New York: Routledge, 1988.

Huyssen, Andreas. *After the Great Divide: Modernism, Mass Culture, Postmodernism*. Bloomington: Indiana UP, 1986.

Jameson, Fredric. Afterword. *Aesthetics and Politics*. London: New Left Books, 1977.

Jitrik, Noé. "Destruction and Forms in Fiction." *Latin America in its Literature*. New York: Holmes & Meier Publishers (1980): 155-180.

Joyce, James. *Ulysses*. Ed. Hans Walter Gabler, et al. New York: Random House, 1986.

Kernan, Alvin. *The Death of Literature*. New Haven: Yale UP, 1990.

Kershner, R.B. *Joyce, Bakhtin, and Popular Literature*. Chapel Hill: U of North Carolina P, 1989.

Kinsella, John. "Realism, Surrealism, and *La casa de cartón*." *Before the Boom: Four Essays on Latin American Literature Before* Liverpool, UK: Centre for Latin-American Studies of the University of Liverpool (1981): 31-39.

Lafuente, Fernando R. "La vanguardia literaria: el escritor como vulgar espantapájaros." *Cuadernos Hispanoamericanos* 2.456-457 (June-July 1988): 937-943.

Larra, Raúl. *Roberto Arlt, el torturado*. Buenos Aires: Editorial Quetzal, 1962.

Larsen, Neil. *Modernism & Hegemony: A Materialist Critique of Aesthetic Agencies*. Minneapolis: U of Minnesota P, 1990.

Lauer, Mirko. *Los exilios interiores: Una introducción a Martín Adán*. Lima: Mosca Azul Editores, 1983.

----, *El sitio de la literatura: Escritores y política en el Perú del siglo XX*. Lima: Mosca Azul Editores, 1989.

Leal, Luis. "El movimiento estridentista." *Los vanguardismos en la América Latina*. Habana: Las Américas (1977): 151-163.

----, "Native and Foreign Influences in Contemporary Mexican Fiction: A Search for Identity." *Tradition and Renewal: Essays on Twentieth Century Latin American Literature and Culture*. Urbana: U of Illinois P (1975): 102-128.

Leland, Christopher Towne. *The Last Happy Men: The Generations of 1922, Fiction, and the Argentine Reality*. Syracuse: Syracuse UP, 1986.

Lindstrom, Naomi. *Twentieth-Century Spanish American Fiction*. Austin: U of Texas P, 1994.

----, "Argentina." *Handbook of Latin American Literature*. David William Foster, Ed. New York: Garland Publishing, Inc., 1987.

Lodge, David. *After Bakhtin: Essays on Fiction and Criticism*. London: Routledge, 1990.

----, *The Modes of Modern Writing: Metaphor, Metonymy, and the Typology of Modern Literature.* London: Edward Arnold Ltd., 1977.

Lyotard, Jean-Francois. "The Postmodern Condition: A Report on Knowledge." *A Postmodern Reader.* Trans. Geoff Bennington and Brian Massumi. Albany: State U of New York P (1993): 71-90.

Masiello, Francine. *Lenguaje e ideología: Las escuelas argentinas de Vanguardia.* Buenos Aires: Librería Hachette, 1986.

Mathews, Tim. "The Machine: Dada, Vorticism and the Future." *The Violent Muse: Violence and the Artistic Imagination in Europe, 1910-1939.* Ed. Jana Howlett and Rod Mengham. Manchester: Manchester UP (1994): 124-140.

McHale, Brian. *Postmodernist Fiction.* New York: Methuen, 1987.

Menton, Seymour. *Latin America's New Historical Novel.* Austin: U of Texas P, 1993.

Murphy, Richard. *Theorizing the Avant-Garde: Modernism, Expressionsim, and the Problem of Postmodernity.* Cambridge, UK: U of Cambridge P, 1999.

Nagel, Susan. *The Influence of the Novels of Jean Giraudoux on the Hispanic Vanguard Novels of the 1920s-1930s.* London: Bucknell UP, 1991.

Ortega y Gasset, José. *Ideas sobre el teatro y la novela.* Madrid: Alianza Editorial, 1982.

Ortega y Gasset, José. *La deshumanización del arte y otros ensayos de estética.* Madrid: Espasa-Calpe, 1987.

Osorio, Nelson. "El estridentismo mexicano y la vanguardia literaria latinoamericana." *Estridentismo: memoria y valoración.* Ed. Esther Hernández Palacios. México: Fondo de Cultura Económica (1983): 49-61.

Palacio, Pablo. *Un hombre muerto a puntapies y Débora.* Santiago de Chile: Editorial Universitaria, 1971.

Pareja Diez Canseco, Alfredo. "El reino de la libertad en Pablo Palacio." *Recopilación de textos sobre Pablo Palacio.* Ed. Reinaldo Castillo. Habana: Casa de las Américas (1987): 97-136.

Pérez Firmat, Gustavo. *Idle Fictions: The Hispanic Vanguard Novel, 1926-1934.* Durham: Duke UP, 1982.

Perloff, Marjorie. *The Futurist Moment: Avant-Garde, Avant-Guerre, and the Language of Rupture.* Chicago: U of Chicago P, 1986.

Picon-Garfield, Evelyn and Ivan A. Schulman. "La estética estraVASANTE de la InNegAusencia o la modernidad de Arqueles Vela." *Nueva revista de filología hispánica* 29.1 (1980): 204-212.

Piglia, Ricardo. *Respiración Artificial.* Bogotá: Tercer Mundo Editores, 1980.

Podestá, Guido A. "An Ethnographic Reproach to the Theory of the Avant-Garde: Modernity and Modernism in Latin America and the Harlem Renaissance." *Modern Language Notes* 106 (1991): 395-422.

Poggioli, Renato. *The Theory of the Avant-Garde.* Trans. Gerald Fitzgerald. Cambridge: Harvard UP, 1968.

Poniatowska, Elena. *Tinísima.* México: Ediciones Era, 1992.

Prada Oropeza, Renato. "Texto y proyección: Los relatos de Arqueles Vela". *Estridentismo: memoria y valoración.* México: Fondo de Cultura Económica (1983): 159-175.

Rehbein, Edna Aguirre. *Vanguardist Techniques in Mexican Prose Fiction: 1923-1962.* Diss. U of Texas at Austin, 1988. Austin: AAC 8816551.

Rivas Iturralde, Vladimiro. *Pablo Palacio: Introducción, selección, notas y comentario de textos.* Quito, Editorial Indoamérica, 1983.

Robles, Humberto E. *La noción de vanguardia en el Ecuador: Recepción, trayectoria, documentos,* Quito: Casa de la Cultura Ecuatoriana, 1989.

Rodríguez Monegal, Emir. "Tradition and Renewal." *Latin America in its Literature.* Ed. César Fernández Moreno, etal. New York: Holmes & Meier Publishers (1972): 87-114.

Rojas, Angel. "Pablo Palacio y la crítica ecuatoriana." *Obras completas de Pablo Palacio.* Quito: Casa de la Cultura Ecuatoriana (1964): 21-37.

Rowe, William. "Liberalism and Authority: The Case of Mario Vargas Llosa." On Edge: The Crisis of Contemporary Latin American Culture. Ed. George Yúdice, etal. Minneapolis: U of Minnesota P (1992): 45-64.

Ruffinelli, Jorge. "Pablo Palacio: Literatura, locura y sociedad." *Revista de Crítica Literaria Latinoamericana* 5.10 (1979): 47-60.

Sábato, Ernesto. *The Writer in the Catastrophe of our Time.* Trans. Asa Zatz. Tulsa: Council Oak Books, 1990.

Sánchez, Luis Alberto. *Introducción crítica a la literatura peruana.* Lima: Editorial P.L. Villanueva, 1974.

Sarlo, Beatriz. *Una modernidad periférica: Buenos Aires 1920-1930.* Buenos Aires: Ediciones Nueva Visión, 1988.

Schneider, Luis Mario. *El estridentismo o una literatura de la estrategia.* México: Ediciones de Bellas Artes, 1970.

----, *Ruptura y continuidad; La literatura mexicana en polémica.* México: Fondo de Cultura Económica, 1975.

Schulman, Ivan A. "Las genealogías secretas de la narrativa: del modernismo a la vanguardia." *Prosa hispánica de vanguardia*. Madrid: Editorial Orígenes (1986): 29-42.

Schwartz, Jorge. *Las vanguardias latinoamericanas*. Madrid: Cátedra, 1991.

Sefchovich, Sara. *México: País de ideas, país de novelas, una sociología de la literatura mexicana*. México: Editorial Grijalbo, 1987.

Shattuck, Roger. *The Banquet Years: The Origins of the Avant-Garde in France*. New York: Vintage Books, 1968 (original ed.1955).

Silver, Katherine. *The Cardboard House*. Saint Paul, Minnesota: Graywolf Press, 1990.

Skidmore, Thomas E. and Peter H. Smith. *Modern Latin America*. New York: Oxford University Press, 1984 (1st ed.).

Sommer, Doris. *Foundational Fictions: The National Romances of Latin America*. Berkeley: U of California P, 1991.

Spivak, Gayatri Chakravorty. "Three Women's Texts and a Critique of Imperialism." *"Race," Writing, and Difference*. Chicago: The U of Chicago P (1985): 262-280.

Stavans, Ilán. "Detectives en Latinoamérica". *Quimera* 73 (January 1988): 24-27.

Steiner, Patricia Owen. *Victoria Ocampo, Writer, Feminist, Woman of the World*. Albuquerque: U of New Mexico P, 1999.

Suleiman, Susan Rubin. *Subversive Intent: Gender, Politics, and the Avant-Garde*. Cambridge: Harvard UP, 1990.

Tamayo Vargas, Augusto. *Literatura peruana*. Lima: Librería Studium, 1977.

Todorov, Tzvetan. *Mikhail Bakhtin: The Dialogical Principle*. Trans. Wlad Godzich. Minneapolis: U of Minnesota P, 1984.

Trinh T. Minh-ha. *Woman Native Other: Writing Postcoloniality and Feminism*. Bloomington: Indiana UP, 1989.

Tyler, Joseph. "El vanguardismo en algunas obras de Julio Cortázar." *Prosa hispánica de vanguardia*. Ed. Fernando Burgos. Madrid: Editorial Orígenes (1986): 163-172.

Unruh, Vicky. *Latin American Vanguards: The Art of Contentious Encounters*. Berkeley: U of California P, 1994.

Vargas Llosa, Mario. "Latin America: Fiction and Reality." *On Modern Latin American Fiction*. New York: Farrar, Straus & Giroux (1987): 1-17.

Vela, Arqueles. *El café de nadie*. Jalapa: Ediciones de Horizonte, 1926.

Verani, Hugo J. *Las vanguardias literarias en Hispanoamérica*. México: Fondo de Cultura Económica, 1990.

Waugh, Patricia. *Metafiction: The Theory and Practice of Self-Conscious Fiction*. London-New York: Methuen, 1984.

Weir, David. *Anachy & Culture, The Aesthetic Politics of Modernism*. Amherst: U of Massachusetts P, 1997.

Weller, Hubert P. *Bibliografía analítica y anotada de y sobre Martín Adán: Rafael de la Fuente Benavides, 1917-1974*. Lima: Instituto Nacional de Cultura, 1975.

Williams, Raymond. "Language and the Avant-Garde." *The Linguistics of Writing: Arguments between Language and Literature*. Manchester: Manchester UP (1987): 33-47.

Yúdice, George. "Postmodernity and Transnational Capitalism in Latin America." *On Edge: The Crisis of Contemporary Latin American Culture*. Minneapolis: U of Minnesota P (1992): 1-28.

Yurkievich, Saúl. "Los avatares de la vanguardia." *Revista Iberoamericana* 48.118-119 (Jan.-June 1982): 351-366.

Index

About the Author

Elizabeth Coonrod Martínez is Associate Professor and Chair of the Department of Modern Languages & Literatures at Sonoma State University in northern California. She received her Ph.D. in Spanish/Latin American Literature from the University of New Mexico in Albuquerque. Martínez has published three biographies of great Hispanics and a history of Mexican-American people in the U.S., for young readers, with the Millbrook Press in Connecticut. Her research and academic publications focus on Mexican and U.S. Latina writers, Latin American early and late twentieth century literature, and Mexican/Central American indigenous civilizations.